Cindy Casciato's

Block
Explosion

Large Scale Fabrics + Fewer Blocks = *Quick & Easy Quilts!*

LEISURE ARTS, INC.
Little Rock, Arkansas

EDITORIAL STAFF

Vice President and Editor-in-Chief: Sandra Graham Case
Executive Director of Publications: Cheryl Nodine Gunnells
Senior Director of Publications: Susan White Sullivan
Director of Designer Relations: Debra Nettles
Senior Design Director: Cyndi Hansen
Editorial Director: Susan Frantz Wiles
Senior Director of Public Relations and Retail Marketing:
Stephen Wilson
Senior Art Operations Director: Jeff Curtis

TECHNICAL/EDITORIAL

Leaflet Publications Director: Mary Hutcheson
Technical Editor: Lisa Lancaster
Technical Writer: Andrea Ahlen
Associate Editor: Steven M. Cooper

ART

Art Publications Director: Rhonda Hodge Shelby
Art Imaging Director: Mark Hawkins
Art Category Manager: Lora Puls
Lead Graphic Designer: Stephanie Hamling
Graphic Designers: Andrea A. Amerson, Karen Allbright,
Laura Adkins, Jennifer Patton, Stephanie Stephens
Imaging Technicians: Steph Johnson and Mark Russell Potter
Staff Photographer: Lloyd Litsey
Photography Stylists: Cassie Newsome and Jan Nobles
Publishing Systems Administrator: Becky Riddle
Publishing Systems Assistants: Clint Hanson,
John Rose, and Chris Wertenberger

BUSINESS STAFF

Publisher: Rick Barton
Vice President, Finance: Tom Siebenmorgen
Director of Corporate Planning and Development:
Laticia Mull Dittrich
Vice President, Retail Marketing: Bob Humphrey
Vice President, Sales: Ray Shelgosh
Vice President, National Accounts: Pam Stebbins
Director of Sales and Services: Margaret Reinold
Vice President, Operations: Jim Dittrich
Comptroller, Operations: Rob Thieme
Retail Customer Service Manager: Stan Raynor
Print Production Manager: Fred F. Pruss

Softcover ISBN 1-57486-448-3

10 9 8 7 6 5 4 3 2 1

Dedication
I dedicate this book to Drew Casciato, my friend, partner and husband, who brings joy into my life. Drew has always encouraged me to pursue my dreams and he's supported me through every endeavor.

TABLE OF CONTENTS

Cindy's Block Explosion Theory	3
Meet the Designer	4
One Patch Frame	6
Prairie Garden	12
Through the Looking Glass	20
Garden Gate	30
Dream Weaver	38
Papa's Plaid	46
Stairway to My Garden	54
Stars and Bars	62
Fancy's Star	70
Flower Patch	78
General Instructions	86

Cindy's Block Explosion Theory:
Large Scale Fabrics + Fewer Blocks = *Quick & Easy Quilts!*

Are you looking for a way to get more out of your quilting time? Would you like to complete a quilt top in a day or a weekend? Then you need to discover Block Explosion quilts! They simply combine classic, traditional blocks "exploded" to a larger scale.

For instance, to make a queen-size quilt top using 12" blocks, you need **35** blocks in a standard 5 by 7 block setting. When you explode the block to a larger scale, say 15", you only need **24** blocks in a 4 by 6 block setting to get a comparable-size quilt top. **That's 11 fewer blocks to sew!** What a timesaver. Cutting and stitching larger blocks means less time needed to complete your quilt top.

Remember those special inspirational fabrics you've saved for just the right quilt design? You know the kind I'm talking about: large floral prints, batiks, theme prints, and novelty fabrics. The large-scale fabric designs cannot really be appreciated when cut into smaller pieces. When the block is exploded to a larger size, the pieces are also much larger. This allows you to use a larger scale print to fill the space without compromising the design.

The Block Explosion concept gives you the opportunity to really enjoy using all those inspirational fabrics you've been collecting.

You do the math. How much time can you save making a Block Explosion quilt?

Block Size	Setting	Full/Queen Size (without borders)	Total Blocks	How many fewer blocks do you have to make?
12"	5 x 7 blocks	60" x 84"	35 blocks	
14"	4 x 6 blocks	56" x 84"	24 blocks	11 blocks
15"	4 x 6 blocks	60" x 90"	24 blocks	11 blocks
16"	4 x 6 blocks	64" x 96"	24 blocks	11 blocks
16"	4 x 5 blocks	64" x 80"	20 blocks	15 blocks
18"	4 x 5 blocks	72" x 90"	20 blocks	15 blocks
18"	3 x 4 blocks	54" x 72"	12 blocks	23 blocks
20"	3 x 4 blocks	60" x 80"	12 blocks	23 blocks

So . . . you can finish faster and showcase those wonderful larger scale prints you love. Let's bring on the Block Explosions!

— *Cindy Casciato*

Meet the Designer

A veteran quilter for more than 25 years, Cindy Casciato understands both the emotional appeal of quilts and the creative side of designing and making them.

She was first exposed to quilting as a little girl when her maternal grandmother presented a quilt to each of her 16 grandchildren. The pattern on Cindy's quilt was a Dutch Girl with a parasol, and she holds many fond memories of that special childhood gift and its creator, Madge May Plunk of Bruce, Mississippi.

"I actually own the treadle sewing machine that my grandmother purchased in 1914 for $21.00," Cindy says. "She was a prolific quilter, making well over 250 quilts in her lifetime. All her patterns were hand drawn on brown paper bags, and she only used the scraps left over from making clothes for her four children. I am very happy to be able to carry on this fine tradition, and I hope to pass on the love of sewing and piecing to my own two daughters, Tara and Virginia."

Today at her home in Ravenna, Ohio, Cindy pursues her love of quilting in a dramatically different fashion from that of her grandmother. Cindy's large studio features a 14-foot counter for cutting and sorting fabric, with storage bins underneath that are filled with brand new fabric divided into the 12 colors of the color wheel. A 12-foot design wall is covered in batting, and there are three sewing machines, two sewing stations where she alternates her sewing activities, and a wall unit for her computer, books, and file storage.

Cindy has been quilting regularly since the late 1970's, after her children were born. "I took a class and made a Log Cabin Quilt," she recalls. "I really enjoyed the whole process, from selecting fabrics to machine piecing and quilting."

Eventually she began teaching quilting at the Stitch, Piece 'n Purl Shop in nearby Cuyahoga Falls. To help serve the classes, she established her own pattern company called Thimble Box in 1990.

An outgoing person who enjoys interaction with other quilters, Cindy founded the Calico Hearts Quilting Guild in Ravenna and served as chairperson of the North East Ohio Quilt Council. She also became a member of the National Quilting Association, the American Quilter's Society, and the American Sewing Guild. Her position as national education specialist, which she held for eight years with Jo-Ann Stores, Inc., was the perfect opportunity to blend business and her passion for quilting.

In the months following the 9/11 terrorist attack on the World Trade Center, Cindy was inspired to create a quilt design as a tribute to firefighters everywhere. The original quilt started out as a gift to her husband, Drew, a firefighter who was injured on the job and was forced to retire. Inscribed with the message, "We will not falter, we will not fear, we will not fail, and we will not forget," Cindy's "American Spirit" quilt was soon made available through Jo-Ann Stores in kit form so that other quilters could express their feelings as well. Individual chapters of the American Sewing Guild all across the United States have since fashioned patriotic wall hangings based on the design and have presented them to their local fire departments.

Cindy is now creating new quilting designs and patterns, organizing annual QuiltEscape retreats, designing fabrics, and developing new products for quilters. She travels throughout the eastern United States as an invitational teacher and lecturer for numerous quilting guilds. Her primary class topics are Color First (gaining confidence in fabric selection), Block Explosion (timesaving techniques and assembly-line piecing), and Studio Time (organizing sewing space to generate more time for quilting).

Cindy says teaching classes and staying in contact with her students helps her to stay focused on current quilting trends and interests. She may be contacted via e-mail at **cindyquilts@neo.rr.com** or through her Web site at **www.QuiltEscape.com.**

This book is Cindy's first Leisure Arts quilt publication. Her designs also have been featured in such popular periodicals as Traditional Quilter, Quilting International, The Professional Quilter (which nominated her for 1996 Teacher of the Year), and The Record Courier.

In addition to their two daughters, Cindy and Drew have two sons, Andrew and Daniel, and a son-in-law, Jason. They love family get-togethers and sharing time with their 5-year-old granddaughter, Amanda, and 2-year-old grandson, Caleb. The Casciatos also enjoy entertaining, swimming, and visiting historical landmarks.

Cindy would like to give a special thanks to the members of the Calico Hearts Quilting Guild of Ravenna, Ohio, for the many hours of personal time they contributed to help complete the quilts in this book. Cindy Casciato (**back row, second from right**) poses with some of her fellow members: (**back row, from left**) Sylvia Kennedy, Claudia Bissler, Gayla Pittman, Jane Griffith, Sandra Phillips, Janis Hittle, and Bonnie Sanford; (**front row, from left**) Mary Kay Hluch, Vivian Kent, and Cathy Byers. Members not shown are Sandra Allan, Helen Cutlip, Judy Drugan, Betty Fitzpatrick, DeLoryes Hicks, Beth Leonard, Debbie Remley, Kathy Schneider, Alma Spaeth, Bonnie Stull, Mary Stull, Annalee Wright, and JoAnn Zeigler.

Dear Quilting Friends,

You can complete a One Patch Frame quilt in about 6 hours. The 12" center block in this design is a good way to show off your fun and exciting inspirational fabric.

In Pieces,

Cindy

One Patch Frame

One Patch *Frame*

	Twin-size
Finished Size	73" x 91" (185 cm x 231 cm)
Block Size	18" x 18" (46 cm x 46 cm)
Number of Blocks	12 blocks
Setting	3 x 4 blocks
Borders	2 borders

YARDAGE
Yardage is based on 45" (114 cm) wide fabric.

Fabric	Twin-size
Large Print	$1^5/8$ yds (1.5 m)
Medium Print	1 yd (91 cm)
Dark Print	$1^3/8$ yds (1.3 m)
Inner Border	$2^1/4$ yds (2.1 m)
Outer Border	$2^3/4$ yds (2.5 m)
Binding	$^3/4$ yd (69 cm)
Backing	$5^1/2$ yds (5.0 m)
Batting	81" x 99" (2.1 m x 2.5 m)

Helpful Hint:

It will be easier to cut out your quilt if you buy the yardage for the blocks and borders separately as listed in the table.

CUTTING OUT THE PIECES

*Follow **Rotary Cutting**, page 87, to cut fabric. All measurements include a ¹/₄" seam allowance. Cut all fabric from the crosswise (selvage to selvage) grain of fabric unless otherwise indicated. Cutting lengths given for borders are exact. You may wish to add an extra 2" of length at each end for "insurance," trimming borders to fit quilt top center.*

Fabric	Twin-size
Large Print	☐ Cut 4 strips (**A**) 12¹/₂" wide for Strip Sets.
Medium Print	☐ Cut 8 strips (**B**) 3¹/₂" wide for Strip Sets. ☐ Cut 1 strip 3¹/₂" wide. From this strip, cut 4 corner squares (**C**) 3¹/₂" x 3¹/₂".
Dark Print	☐ Cut 12 strips 3¹/₂" wide. From these strips, cut 24 rectangles (**D**) 3¹/₂" x 18¹/₂".
Inner Border	☐ Cut 2 lengthwise inner top/bottom borders (**E**) 3¹/₂" x 54¹/₂". ☐ Cut 2 lengthwise inner side borders (**F**) 3¹/₂" x 72¹/₂".
Outer Border	☐ Cut 2 lengthwise outer top/bottom borders (**G**) 6¹/₂" x 60¹/₂". ☐ Cut 2 lengthwise outer side borders (**H**) 6¹/₂" x 90¹/₂".
Binding	☐ Cut 9 strips 2¹/₂" wide.

MAKING THE BLOCKS

*Follow **Piecing** and **Pressing**, pages 87-88, to make the blocks. Use a ¹/₄" seam allowance for all seams.*

1 Sew 1 medium print strip (**B**) to each side of large print strip (**A**) as shown to make **Strip Set**. Make 4 **Strip Sets**. Cut across **Strip Sets** at 12¹/₂" intervals to make **Unit 1**. Make 12 **Unit 1's**.

2 Sew a dark print rectangle (**D**) to each side of **Unit 1** as shown to make **Block**. Make 12 **Blocks**.

Strip Set (make 4)   **Unit 1** (make 12)

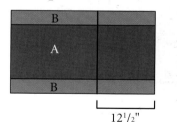
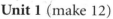

12¹/₂"

Block Diagram (make 12)

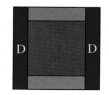

ASSEMBLING THE QUILT TOP

*Refer to **Quilt Top Diagram** and photo, page 11, for placement.*

1 Sew 3 **Blocks** together as shown to make **Row 1**. Make 2 **Row 1's**.

2 Sew 3 **Blocks** together as shown to make **Row 2**. Make 2 **Row 2's**.

3 Alternating rows, sew **Rows 1** and **2** together as shown to make **Quilt Top Center**.

ADDING THE BORDERS

1 Sew 2 inner top/bottom borders (**E**) to **Quilt Top Center**.

2 Sew a medium print square (**C**) to each end of inner side borders (**F**) to make 2 **Border Units**.

3 Sew a **Border Unit** to each side of **Quilt Top Center**.

4 Sew 2 outer top/bottom borders (**G**), then 2 outer side borders (**H**) to pieced center to make **Quilt Top**.

Row 1 (make 2)

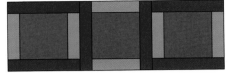

Row 2 (make 2)

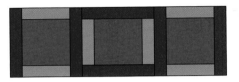

Quilt Top Diagram

COMPLETING THE QUILT

1 Follow **Quilting**, page 89, to mark, layer, and quilt as desired. Our quilt was machine quilted.

2 Follow **Making Straight Grain Binding**, page 93, to make 9½ yds of 2½" wide binding.

3 Follow **Attaching Binding with Mitered Corners**, page 93, to attach binding to quilt.

Dear Quilting Friends,

These Prairie Garden quilts are "sew" easy to piece. Start with your inspiration fabric, add a little accent, and mix them with a light background — simply lovely!

In Pieces,

Cindy

Prairie *Garden*

Prairie Garden

	Wall Hanging	Queen-size
Finished Size	53" x 53" (135 cm x 135 cm)	89" x 121" (226 cm x 307 cm)
Block Size	16" x 16" (41 cm x 41 cm)	16" x 16" (41 cm x 41 cm)
Number of Blocks	4 blocks	24 blocks
Number Of Borders	2 borders	2 borders
Setting	2 x 2 blocks	4 x 6 blocks

YARDAGE

Yardage is based on 45" (114 cm) wide fabric.

Fabric	Wall Hanging
Large Print	5/8 yd (57 cm)
Light Print	3/4 yd (69 cm)
Inner Border	1 yd (91 cm)
Outer Border	1 5/8 yds (1.5 m)
Binding	1/2 yd (46 cm)
Backing	3 1/2 yds (3.2 m)
Batting	61" x 61" (1.5 m x 1.5 m)

Fabric	Queen-size
Large Print	2 1/2 yds (2.3 m)
Light Print	4 yds (3.7 m)
Inner Border	
Light Print	1 3/8 yds (1.3 m)
Pink Print	3/4 yd (69 cm)
Green Print	7/8 yd (80 cm)
Outer Border	3 1/4 yds (3.0 m)
Binding	1 yd (91 cm)
Backing	8 1/8 yds (7.4 m)
Batting	97" x 129" (2.5 m x 3.3 m)

CUTTING OUT THE PIECES

*Follow **Rotary Cutting**, page 87, to cut fabric. All measurements include a ¼" seam allowance. Cut all fabric from the crosswise (selvage to selvage) grain of fabric unless otherwise indicated. Cutting lengths given for borders are exact. You may wish to add an extra 2" of length at each end for "insurance," trimming borders to fit quilt top center.*

Fabric	Wall Hanging	Queen-size
Large Print	☐ Cut 3 strips (**A**) 4½" wide for Strip Sets A and B. ☐ Cut 1 strip 4½" wide. From this strip, cut 4 corner squares (**B**) 4½" x 4½".	☐ Cut 18 strips (**A**) 4½" wide for Strip Sets A and B.
Light Print	☐ Cut 1 strip (**C**) 8½" wide for Strip Set A. ☐ Cut 1 strip (**D**) 4½" wide for Strip Set B. ☐ Cut 1 strip 8½" wide. From this strip, cut 8 rectangles (**E**) 8½" x 4½".	☐ Cut 6 strips (**C**) 8½" wide for Strip Set A. ☐ Cut 6 strips (**D**) 4½" wide for Strip Set B. ☐ Cut 6 strips 8½" wide. From these strips, cut 48 rectangles (**E**) 8½" x 4½".
Inner Border	☐ Cut 4 lengthwise borders (**F**) 4½" x 32½".	☐ From **light print** fabric, cut 5 strips 8½" wide. From these strips, cut 40 rectangles (**F**) 8½" x 4½" for flying geese units. ☐ From **pink print** fabric, cut 5 strips 4½" wide. From these strips, cut 40 squares (**G**) 4½" x 4½" for flying geese units. ☐ From **green print** fabric, cut 6 strips 4½" wide. From these strips, cut 40 squares (**H**) 4½" x 4½" for flying geese units and 4 squares (**B**) 4½" x 4½" for corner squares.
Outer Border	☐ Cut 2 lengthwise side borders (**G**) 6½" x 40½". ☐ Cut 2 lengthwise top/bottom borders (**H**) 6½" x 52½".	☐ Cut 2 lengthwise side borders (**I**) 8½" x 104½". ☐ Cut 2 lengthwise top/bottom borders (**J**) 8½" x 88½".
Binding	☐ Cut 6 strips 2½" wide.	☐ Cut 11 strips 2½" wide.

MAKING THE BLOCKS

*Follow **Piecing** and **Pressing**, pages 87-88, to make the blocks. Use a ¹/₄" seam allowance for all seams.*

1 Sew 2 large print strips (**A**) and 1 light print strip (**C**) together as shown to make **Strip Set A**. For **wall hanging**, make **1 Strip Set A**. Cut across **Strip Set A** at 4¹/₂" intervals to make **8 Unit 1's**. For **queen-size** quilt, make **6 Strip Set A's**. Cut across **Strip Set A's** at 4¹/₂" intervals to make **48 Unit 1's**.

2 Sew 1 large print strip (**A**) and 1 light print strip (**D**) together as shown to make **Strip Set B**. For **wall hanging**, make **1 Strip Set B**. Cut across **Strip Set B** at 4¹/₂" intervals to make **8 Unit 2's**. For **queen-size** quilt, make **6 Strip Set B's**. Cut across **Strip Set B's** at 4¹/₂" intervals to make **48 Unit 2's**.

3 Alternating colors, sew 2 **Unit 2's** together as shown to make **Unit 3**. For **wall hanging**, make **4 Unit 3's**. For **queen-size** quilt, make **24 Unit 3's**.

4 Sew 1 **Unit 3** and 2 light print rectangles (**E**) together as shown to make **Unit 4**. For **wall hanging**, make **4 Unit 4's**. For **queen-size** quilt, make **24 Unit 4's**.

5 Sew 1 **Unit 4** and 2 **Unit 1's** together as shown to make **Block**. For **wall hanging**, make **4 Blocks**. For **queen-size** quilt, make **24 Blocks**.

Strip Set A

4¹/₂"

Unit 1

Strip Set B

4¹/₂"

Unit 2

Unit 3

Unit 4

Block Diagram

ASSEMBLING THE QUILT TOP

Refer to **Quilt Top Diagrams**, *pages 17-18,
for placement.*

Wall Hanging

1 For **wall hanging**, sew 2 **Blocks** together as
shown to make a **Row**. Make **2 Rows**.

2 Sew **Rows** together to make **Quilt Top Center**.

Queen-size Quilt

1 For **queen-size** quilt, sew **4 Blocks** together as
shown to make a **Row**. Make **6 Rows**.

2 Sew **Rows** together to make **Quilt Top Center**.

ADDING THE BORDERS

Wall Hanging

1 Sew inner border (**F**) to each side of
Quilt Top Center.

2 Sew a corner square (**B**) to each end of
remaining inner borders (**F**) to make 2
Border Units. Sew a **Border Unit**
to top and bottom of **Quilt Top Center**.

3 Sew outer side borders (**G**), then outer
top/bottom borders (**H**) to pieced center to
make **Quilt Top**.

Wall Hanging Row

Queen-size Quilt Row

Wall Hanging Top Diagram

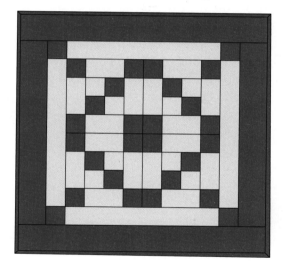

Queen-size Quilt

1 Follow **Making Flying Geese**, page 88, using light print rectangles (**F**), pink print squares (**G**), and green print squares (**H**) to make 20 **Unit 5's** and 20 **Unit 6's**.

2 Sew 6 **Unit 5's** and 6 **Unit 6's** together as shown to make **Side Border**. Make 2 **Inner Side Borders**.

3 Sew 2 corner squares (**B**), 4 **Unit 5's**, and 4 **Unit 6's** together as shown to make **Inner Top Border**. Repeat to make **Inner Bottom Border**.

4 Sew **Inner Side Borders**, then **Inner Top/Bottom Borders** to **Quilt Top Center**.

5 Sew outer side borders (**I**), then outer top/bottom borders (**J**) to pieced center to make **Quilt Top**.

Unit 5 (make 20)   **Unit 6** (make 20)

Inner Side Border   **Inner Top/Bottom Border**

Queen-Size Quilt Top Diagram

COMPLETING THE QUILT

1 Follow **Quilting**, page 89, to mark, layer, and quilt as desired. Our quilt was machine quilted.

2 Follow **Making Straight Grain Binding**, page 93, to make the binding.
For **wall hanging**, make **6¹/₄ yds** of 2¹/₂" wide binding.
For **queen-size** quilt, make **12 yds** of 2¹/₂" wide binding.

3 Follow **Making a Hanging Sleeve**, page 92, to make and attach a hanging sleeve to quilt, if desired.

4 Follow **Attaching Binding with Mitered Corners**, page 93, to attach binding to quilt.

Queen-Size Quilt

Dear Quilting Friends,

The 16" blocks of the Through the Looking Glass quilts will show off your inspiration fabrics and allow you to add three accent fabrics plus a light background fabric.

In Pieces,

Cindy

Through the Looking Glass

Through the Looking Glass

	Wall Hanging	Queen-size
Finished Size	47" x 47" (119 cm x 119 cm)	91" x 123" (231 cm x 312 cm)
Block Size	approx. 16" x 16" (41 cm x 41 cm)	approx. 16" x 16" (41 cm x 41 cm)
Number of Blocks	4 blocks	24 blocks
Number Of Borders	2 borders	3 borders
Setting	2 x 2 blocks	4 x 6 blocks

YARDAGE
Yardage is based on 45" (114 cm) wide fabric.

Fabric	Wall Hanging	Queen-size
Large Print	$3/8$ yd (34 cm)	$1^1/2$ yds (1.4 m)
White Print	$1/2$ yd (46 cm)	2 yds (1.8 m)
Purple Print	$3/8$ yd (34 cm)	$1^1/4$ yds (1.1 m)
Lavender Print	$3/8$ yd (34cm)	$7/8$ yd (80 cm)
Green Print	$3/8$ yd (34 cm)	$1^1/2$ yds (1.4 m)
Inner Border	$1^1/8$ yds (1.0 m)	3 yds (2.7 m)
Middle Border	None	$3^1/8$ yds (2.9 m)
Outer Border	$1^1/2$ yds (1.4 m)	$3^3/8$ yds (3.1 m)
Binding	$1/2$ yd (46 cm)	1 yd (91 cm)
Backing	$3^1/8$ yds (2.9 m)	11 yds (10.1 m)
Batting	55" x 55" (1.4 m x 1.4 m)	99" x 131" (2.5 m x 3.3 m)

CUTTING OUT THE PIECES

*Follow **Rotary Cutting**, page 87, to cut fabric. All measurements include a ¼" seam allowance. Cut all fabric from the crosswise (selvage to selvage) grain of fabric unless otherwise indicated. Cutting lengths given for borders are exact. You may wish to add an extra 2" of length at each end for "insurance," trimming borders to fit quilt top center.*

Fabric	Wall-Hanging	Queen-size
Large Print	☐ Cut 1 strip 11½" wide. From this strip, cut 2 squares 11½" x 11½". Cut each square once diagonally to make 4 triangles (**A**).	☐ Cut 4 strips 11½" wide. From these strips, cut 12 squares 11½" x 11½". Cut each square once diagonally to make 24 triangles (**A**).
White Print	☐ Cut 1 strip (**B**) 6⅛" wide for triangle-squares. ☐ Cut 1 strip 6⅛" wide. From this strip, cut 4 squares 6⅛" x 6⅛". Cut squares once diagonally to make 8 triangles (**C**).	☐ Cut 6 strips (**B**) 6⅛" wide for triangle-squares. ☐ Cut 4 strips 6⅛" wide. From these strips, cut 24 squares 6⅛" x 6⅛". Cut squares once diagonally to make 48 triangles (**C**).
Purple Print	☐ Cut 1 strip (**D**) 6⅛" wide for triangle-squares.	☐ Cut 6 strips (**D**) 6⅛" wide for triangle-squares.
Lavender Print	☐ Cut 1 strip 6⅛" wide. From this strip, cut 4 squares 6⅛" x 6⅛". Cut squares once diagonally to make 8 triangles (**E**).	☐ Cut 4 strips 6⅛" wide. From these strips, cut 24 squares 6⅛" x 6⅛". Cut squares once diagonally to make 48 triangles (**E**).
Green Print	☐ Cut 1 strip 11½" wide. From this strip, cut 2 squares 11½" x 11½". Cut each square once diagonally to make 4 triangles (**F**).	☐ Cut 4 strips 11½" wide. From these strips, cut 12 squares 11½" x 11½". Cut squares once diagonally to make 24 triangles (**F**).
Inner Border	☐ Cut 2 lengthwise side borders (**G**) 2½" x 32½". ☐ Cut 2 lengthwise top/bottom borders (**H**) 2½" x 36½".	☐ Cut 2 lengthwise side borders (**G**) 2½" x 96½". ☐ Cut 2 lengthwise top/bottom borders (**H**) 2½" x 68½".
Middle Border	None	☐ Cut 2 lengthwise side borders (**I**) 4½" x 100½". ☐ Cut 2 lengthwise top/bottom borders (**J**) 4½" x 76½".
Outer Border	☐ Cut 2 lengthwise side borders (**I**) 5½" x 36½". ☐ Cut 2 lengthwise top/bottom borders (**J**) 5½" x 46½".	☐ Cut 2 lengthwise side borders (**K**) 7½" x 108½". ☐ Cut 2 lengthwise top/bottom borders (**L**) 7½" x 90½".
Binding	☐ Cut 5 strips 2½" wide.	☐ Cut 11 strips 2½" wide.

MAKING THE BLOCKS

*Follow **Piecing** and **Pressing**, pages 87-88, to make the blocks. Use a ¹/₄" seam allowance for all seams.*

1 Matching right sides and raw edges, stack each white print strip (**B**) on a purple print strip (**D**) as shown in **Fig. 1**.
For **wall hanging**, make **1** layered strip.
Cut layered strip at 6¹/₈" intervals to make **6 Unit 1** squares. Do not separate squares.
For **queen-size** quilt, make **6** layered strips.
Cut layered strips at 6¹/₈" intervals to make **36 Unit 1** squares. Do not separate squares.

2 Draw a diagonal line (corner to corner) on wrong side of each white print **Unit 1** square. Stitch seam ¹/₄" from each side of drawn line (**Fig. 2**). Trim along drawn line and press open to make 2 **Unit 2** triangle-squares.
For **wall hanging**, make **12 Unit 2's.**
For **queen-size** quilt, make **72 Unit 2's.**

3 Sew 1 **Unit 2** and 1 lavender triangle (**E**) together as shown to make **Unit 3**.
For **wall hanging**, make **4 Unit 3's.**
For **queen-size** quilt, make **24 Unit 3's.**

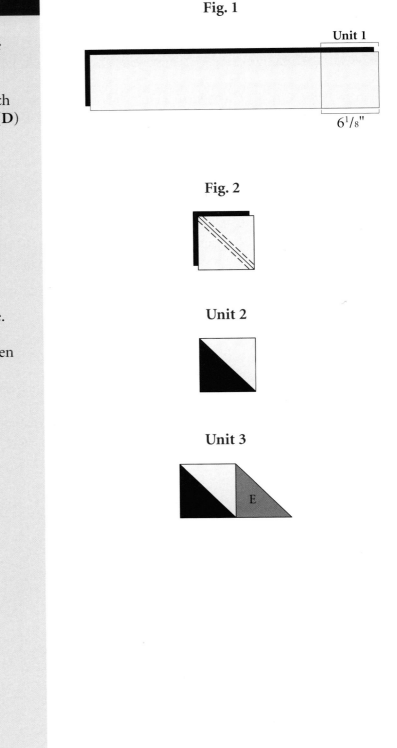

Fig. 1

Unit 1

6¹/₈"

Fig. 2

Unit 2

Unit 3

E

4 Sew 1 **Unit 2**, 1 lavender triangle (**E**), and 1 white triangle (**C**) together as shown to make **Unit 4**.
For **wall hanging**, make **4 Unit 4's**.
For **queen-size** quilt, make **24 Unit 4's**.

5 Sew 1 **Unit 2** and 1 white triangle (**C**) together as shown to make **Unit 5**.
For **wall hanging**, make **4 Unit 5's**.
For **queen-size** quilt, make **24 Unit 5's**.

6 Sew **Unit 3**, **Unit 4**, and **Unit 5** together as shown to make **Unit 6**.
For **wall hanging**, make **4 Unit 6's**.
For **queen-size** quilt, make **24 Unit 6's**.

7 Sew **Unit 6**, green print triangle (**F**), and large print triangle (**A**) together as shown to make **Block**.
For **wall hanging**, make **4 Blocks**.
For **queen-size** quilt, make **24 Blocks**.

Unit 4

Unit 5

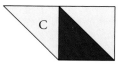

Unit 6

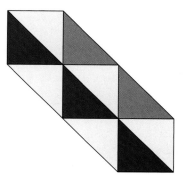

Block Diagram

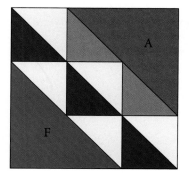

ASSEMBLING THE QUILT TOP

*Refer to **Quilt Top Diagrams**, page 27, and photos, pages 28-29, for placement.*

Wall Hanging

1 Sew **2 Blocks** together as shown to make a **Row**. Make **2 Rows**.

2 Sew **Rows** together to make **Wall Hanging Top Center**.

Queen-size Quilt

1 Sew **4 Blocks** together as shown to make a **Row**. Make **6 Rows**.

2 Sew **Rows** together to make **Quilt Top Center**.

Wall Hanging Row

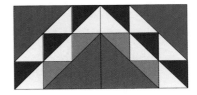

Queen-size Quilt Row

ADDING THE BORDERS

Wall Hanging

1 Sew inner side borders (**G**), then inner top/bottom borders (**H**) to **Quilt Top Center**.

2 Sew outer side borders (**I**), then outer top/bottom borders (**J**) to pieced center to make **Quilt Top**.

Queen-size Quilt

1 Sew inner side borders (**G**), then inner top/bottom borders (**H**) to **Quilt Top Center**.

2 Sew middle side borders (**I**), then middle top/bottom borders (**J**) to pieced center.

3 Sew outer side borders (**K**), then outer top/bottom borders (**L**) to pieced center to make **Quilt Top**.

Wall Hanging Top Diagram

Queen-size Quilt Top Diagram

COMPLETING THE QUILT

1 Follow **Quilting**, page 89, to mark, layer, and quilt as desired. Our quilt was machine quilted.

2 Follow **Making Straight Grain Binding**, page 93, to make the binding.
For **wall hanging**, make **5⁵/₈ yds** of 2¹/₂" wide binding.
For **queen-size** quilt, make **12¹/₄ yds** of 2¹/₂" wide binding.

3 Follow **Making a Hanging Sleeve**, page 92, to make and attach a hanging sleeve to quilt, if desired.

4 Follow **Attaching Binding with Mitered Corners**, page 93, to attach binding to quilt.

Wall Hanging

Queen-size Quilt

Dear Quilting Friends,

The Garden Gate quilt is "sew" much fun and "sew" fast to make. You can assemble these blocks from strip sets combining three fabrics — or get really creative and use up your scraps for a one-of- a-kind quilt!

In Pieces,

Cindy

Garden *Gate*

Garden Gate

	Lap-size	Queen-size
Finished Size	58" x 58" (147 cm x 147 cm)	87" x 102" (221 cm x 259 cm)
Block Size	15" x 15" (38 cm x 38 cm)	15" x 15" (38 cm x 38 cm)
Number of Blocks	9 blocks	20 blocks
Number Of Borders	2 borders	3 borders
Setting	3 x 3 blocks	4 x 5 blocks

YARDAGE

Yardage is based on 45" (114 cm) wide fabric.

Fabric	Lap-size	Queen-size
Large Print	$1^1/_2$ yds (1.4 m) **total** of assorted prints	$2^7/_8$ yds (2.6 m)
Light Print	None	$1^5/_8$ yds (1.5 m)
Dark Print	$^3/_4$ yd (69 cm)	$^3/_8$ yd (34 cm)
Inner Border	$1^1/_2$ yds (1.4 m)	$2^1/_2$ yds (2.3 m)
Middle Border	None	$2^1/_2$ yds (2.3 m)
Outer Border	$1^3/_4$ yds (1.6 m)	$3^1/_8$ yds (2.9 m)
Binding	$^5/_8$ yd (57 cm)	$^7/_8$ yd (80 cm)
Backing	$3^3/_4$ yds (3.4 m)	8 yds (7.3 m)
Batting	66" x 66" (1.7 m x 1.7 m)	95" x 110" (2.4 m x 2.8 m)

Helpful Hint:

Assembly line sewing will really speed up the process when making blocks.

CUTTING OUT THE PIECES

*Follow **Rotary Cutting**, page 87, to cut fabric. All measurements include a ¹/₄" seam allowance. Cut all fabric from the crosswise (selvage to selvage) grain of fabric unless otherwise indicated. Cutting lengths given for borders are exact. You may wish to add an extra 2" of length at each end for "insurance," trimming borders to fit quilt top center.*

Fabric	Lap-size	Queen-size
Large Print	☐ Cut 36 assorted squares (**A**) 6¹/₂" x 6¹/₂". ☐ Cut 1 strip (**D**) 3¹/₂" wide for Strip Set B. ☐ Cut 1 strip 3¹/₂" wide. From this strip, cut 4 corner squares (**E**) 3¹/₂" x 3¹/₂".	☐ Cut 14 strips (**A**) 6¹/₂" wide for Strip Set A.
Light Print	None	☐ Cut 7 strips (**B**) 3¹/₂" wide for Strip Set A. ☐ Cut 4 strips (**C**) 6¹/₂" wide for Strip Set B.
Dark Print	☐ Cut 3 strips 3¹/₂" wide. From these strips, cut 18 rectangles (**B**) 3¹/₂" x 6¹/₂". ☐ Cut 2 strips (**C**) 6¹/₂" wide for Strip Set B.	☐ Cut 2 strips (**D**) 3¹/₂" wide for Strip Set B. ☐ Cut 1 strip 3¹/₂" wide. From this strip, cut 4 corner squares (**E**) 3¹/₂" x 3¹/₂".
Inner Border	☐ Cut 4 lengthwise borders (**F**) 3¹/₂" x 45¹/₂".	☐ Cut 2 lengthwise top/bottom borders (**F**) 3¹/₂" x 60¹/₂". ☐ Cut 2 lengthwise side borders (**G**) 3¹/₂" x 81¹/₂".
Middle Border	None	☐ Cut 2 lengthwise top/bottom borders (**H**) 3¹/₂" x 66¹/₂". ☐ Cut 2 lengthwise side borders (**I**) 3¹/₂" x 81¹/₂".
Outer Border	☐ Cut 2 lengthwise top/bottom borders (**G**) 3¹/₂" x 51¹/₂". ☐ Cut 2 lengthwise side borders (**H**) 3¹/₂" x 57¹/₂". **Note:** Our quilt was made with pieced borders using random lengths of 3¹/₂" wide large print strips.	☐ Cut 2 lengthwise top/bottom borders (**J**) 7¹/₂" x 72¹/₂". ☐ Cut 2 lengthwise side borders (**K**) 7¹/₂" x 101¹/₂".
Binding	☐ Cut 7 strips 2¹/₂" wide.	☐ Cut 10 strips 2¹/₂" wide.

MAKING THE BLOCKS

*Follow **Piecing** and **Pressing**, pages 87-88, to make the blocks. Use a ¹/₄" seam allowance for all seams.*

1 For **lap-size** quilt, sew 2 large print squares (**A**) and 1 dark print rectangle (**B**) together to make **Unit 1**. Make **18 Unit 1's**.
For **queen-size** quilt, sew 2 large print strips (**A**) and 1 light print strip (**B**) together as shown to make **Strip Set A**. Make **7 Strip Set A's**. Cut across **Strip Set A's** at 6¹/₂" intervals to make **Unit 1**. Make **40 Unit 1's**.

2 For **lap-size** quilt, sew 2 dark print strips (**C**) and 1 large print strip (**D**) together to make **Strip Set B**. Make **1 Strip Set B**. Cut across **Strip Set B** at 3¹/₂" intervals to make **9 Unit 2's**.
For **queen-size** quilt, sew 2 light print strips (**C**) and 1 dark print strip (**D**) together as shown to make **Strip Set B**. Make **2 Strip Set B's**. Cut across **Strip Set B's** at 3¹/₂" intervals to make **20 Unit 2's**.

3 Sew 2 **Unit 1's** and 1 **Unit 2** together as shown to make **Block**.
For **lap-size** quilt, make **9 Blocks**.
For **queen-size** quilt, make **20 Blocks**.

ASSEMBLING THE QUILT TOP

*Refer to **Quilt Top Diagrams**, page 35, for placement.*

Lap-size Quilt

1 For **lap-size** quilt, sew **3 Blocks** together to make a **Row**. Make **3 Rows**.

2 Sew **Rows** together to make **Quilt Top Center**.

Strip Set A (make 7)   **Unit 1**

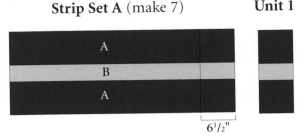

6¹/₂"

Strip Set B   **Unit 2**

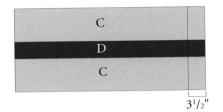

3¹/₂"

Block Diagram

Queen-size Quilt

1 For **queen-size** quilt, sew **4 Blocks** together to make a **Row**. Make **5 Rows**.

2 Sew **Rows** together to make **Quilt Top Center**.

ADDING THE BORDERS

Lap-size Quilt

1 Sew 2 inner borders (**F**) to top and bottom of **Quilt Top Center**.

2 Sew 1 corner square (**E**) to each end of remaining inner borders (**F**) to make 2 **Border Units**.

3 Sew 1 **Border Unit** to each side of pieced center.

4 Sew outer top/bottom borders (**G**), then outer side borders (**H**) to pieced center to make **Quilt Top**.

Queen-size Quilt

1 Sew inner top/bottom borders (**F**), then inner side borders (**G**) to **Quilt Top Center**.

2 Sew middle side borders (**I**) to pieced center.

3 Sew 1 corner square (**E**) to each end of middle top/bottom borders (**H**) to make 2 **Border Units**.

4 Sew 1 **Border Unit** to top and bottom of pieced center.

5 Sew outer top/bottom borders (**J**), then outer side borders (**K**) to pieced center to make **Quilt Top**.

Lap-size Quilt Top Diagram

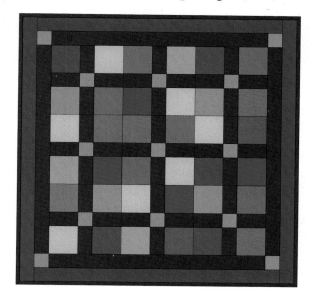

Queen-size Quilt Top Diagram

COMPLETING THE QUILT

1 Follow **Quilting**, page 89, to mark, layer, and quilt as desired. Our quilts were machine quilted.

2 Follow **Making Straight Grain Binding**, page 93, to make the binding. For **lap-size** quilt, make **6³/₄ yds** of 2¹/₂" wide binding.

For **queen-size** quilt, make **10⁷/₈ yds** of 2¹/₂" wide binding.

3 Follow **Attaching Binding with Mitered Corners**, page 93, to attach binding to quilt.

Lap-size Quilt

Queen-size Quilt

Dear Quilting Friends,

This quilt only takes 16 blocks to make a queen-size quilt or just 4 blocks to make a matching wall hanging! The color placement in the block creates an all-over woven design.

In Pieces,

Cindy

Dream Weaver

Dream Weaver

	Wall Hanging	Queen-size
Finished Size	43" x 43" (109 cm x 109 cm)	91" x 91" (231 cm x 231 cm)
Block Size	15" x 15" (38 cm x 38 cm)	15" x 15" (38 cm x 38 cm)
Number of Blocks	4 blocks	16 blocks
Number Of Borders	2 borders	3 borders
Setting	2 x 2 blocks	4 x 4 blocks

YARDAGE

Yardage is based on 45" (114 cm) wide fabric.

Fabric	Wall Hanging	Queen-size
Large Print	$3/8$ yd (34 cm)	$1^1/4$ yds (1.1 m)
Gold Print	$5/8$ yd (57 cm)	$1^1/2$ yds (1.4 m)
Purple Print	$3/8$ yd (34 cm)	1 yd (91 cm)
Plum Print	$1/4$ yd (23 cm)	$5/8$ yd (57 cm)
Inner Border	$1^1/8$ yds (1.0 m)	$2^1/8$ yds (1.9 m)
Middle Border	None	$2^3/8$ yds (2.2 m)
Outer Border	$1^3/8$ yds (1.3 m)	$2^7/8$ yds (2.6 m)
Binding	$1/2$ yd (46 cm)	$7/8$ yd (80 cm)
Backing	$2^7/8$ yds (2.6 m)	$8^1/4$ yds (7.5 m)
Batting	51" x 51" (1.3 m x 1.3 m)	99" x 99" (2.5 m x 2.5 m)

CUTTING OUT THE PIECES

*Follow **Rotary Cutting**, page 87, to cut fabric. All measurements include a $1/4$" seam allowance. Cut all strips from the crosswise (selvage to selvage) grain of fabric unless otherwise indicated. Cutting lengths given for borders are exact. You may wish to add an extra 2" of length at each end for "insurance," trimming borders to fit quilt top center.*

Fabric	Wall Hanging	Queen-size
Large Print	☐ Cut 2 strips $5^1/2$" wide. From these strips, cut 12 squares (**A**) $5^1/2$" x $5^1/2$".	☐ Cut 7 strips $5^1/2$" wide. From these strips, cut 48 squares (**A**) $5^1/2$" x $5^1/2$".
Gold Print	☐ Cut 3 strips (**B**) 6" wide for triangle-squares.	☐ Cut 8 strips (**B**) 6" wide for triangle-squares.
Purple Print	☐ Cut 2 strips (**C**) 6" wide for triangle-squares.	☐ Cut 5 strips (**C**) 6" wide for triangle-squares.
Plum Print	☐ Cut 1 strip (**D**) 6" wide for triangle-squares.	☐ Cut 3 strips (**D**) 6" wide for triangle-squares.
Inner Border	☐ Cut 2 lengthwise side borders (**E**) $2^1/2$" x $30^1/2$". ☐ Cut 2 lengthwise top/bottom borders (**F**) $2^1/2$" x $34^1/2$".	☐ Cut 2 lengthwise side borders (**E**) $3^1/2$" x $60^1/2$". ☐ Cut 2 lengthwise top/bottom borders (**F**) $3^1/2$" x $66^1/2$".
Middle Border	None	☐ Cut 2 lengthwise side borders (**G**) $5^1/2$" x $66^1/2$". ☐ Cut 2 lengthwise top/bottom borders (**H**) $5^1/2$" x $76^1/2$".
Outer Border	☐ Cut 2 lengthwise side borders (**G**) $4^1/2$" x $34^1/2$". ☐ Cut 2 lengthwise top/bottom borders (**H**) $4^1/2$" x $42^1/2$".	☐ Cut 2 lengthwise side borders (**I**) $7^1/2$" x $76^1/2$". ☐ Cut 2 lengthwise top/bottom borders (**J**) $7^1/2$" x $90^1/2$".
Binding	☐ Cut 5 strips $2^1/2$" wide.	☐ Cut 10 strips $2^1/2$" wide.

MAKING THE BLOCKS

*Follow **Piecing** and **Pressing**, pages 87-88, to make the blocks. Use a 1/4" seam allowance for all seams.*

1 Matching right sides and raw edges, stack a gold print strip (**B**) on a purple print strip (**C**) as shown in **Fig. 1**.
For **wall hanging**, make **2** layered strips. Cut layered strips at 6" intervals to make **8 Unit 1** layered squares. Do not separate squares. For **queen-size** quilt, make **5** layered strips. Cut layered strips at 6" intervals to make **32 Unit 1** layered squares. Do not separate squares.

2 Draw a diagonal line (corner to corner) on wrong side of each gold print **Unit 1** square. Stitch seam 1/4" from each side of drawn line (**Fig. 2**). Trim along drawn line and press open to make 2 **Unit 2** triangle-squares. Trim **Unit 2's** to measure 5 1/2" x 5 1/2".
For **wall hanging**, make **16 Unit 2's**.
For **queen-size** quilt, make **64 Unit 2's**.

3 Follow Steps 1 and 2 to make **Unit 4** triangle-squares using remaining gold print strips (**B**) and plum print strips (**D**) as shown in **Figs. 3** and **4**. Trim **Unit 4's** to measure 5 1/2" x 5 1/2".
For **wall hanging**, make **8 Unit 4's**.
For **queen-size** quilt, make **32 Unit 4's**.

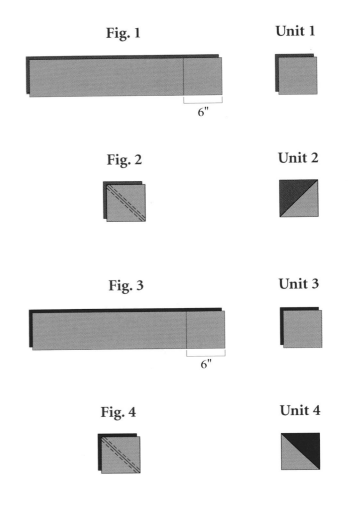

Fig. 1   Unit 1   6"

Fig. 2   Unit 2

Fig. 3   Unit 3   6"

Fig. 4   Unit 4

4 Sew 1 large print square (**A**), 1 **Unit 2**, and 1 **Unit 4** together as shown to make **Unit 5**. For **wall hanging**, make **8 Unit 5's**. For **queen-size** quilt, make **32 Unit 5's**.

5 Sew 1 large print square (**A**) and 2 **Unit 2's** together as shown to make **Unit 6**. For **wall hanging**, make **4 Unit 6's**. For **queen-size** quilt, make **16 Unit 6's**.

6 Sew 2 **Unit 5's** and 1 **Unit 6** together as shown to make **Block**. For **wall hanging**, make **4 Blocks**. For **queen-size** quilt, make **16 Blocks**.

ASSEMBLING THE QUILT TOP

*Refer to **Quilt Top Diagrams**, page 44, for placement.*

Wall Hanging

1 Sew **2 Blocks** together as shown to make a **Row**. Make **2 Rows**.

2 Sew **Rows** together to make **Quilt Top Center**.

Queen-size

1 Sew **4 Blocks** together as shown to make a **Row**. Make **4 Rows**.

2 Sew **Rows** together to make **Quilt Top Center**.

Unit 5

Unit 6

Block Diagram

Wall Hanging

Queen-size Quilt Row

ADDING THE BORDERS

Wall Hanging

1 Sew inner side borders (**E**), then inner top/bottom borders (**F**) to **Quilt Top Center**.

2 Sew outer side borders (**G**), then outer top/bottom borders (**H**) to pieced center to make **Quilt Top**.

Queen-size Quilt

1 Sew inner side borders (**E**), then inner top/bottom borders (**F**) to **Quilt Top Center**.

2 Sew middle side borders (**G**), then middle top/bottom borders (**H**) to pieced center.

3 Sew outer side borders (**I**), then outer top/bottom borders (**J**) to pieced center to make **Quilt Top**.

Wall Hanging Top Diagram

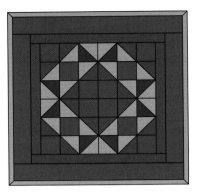

Queen-size Quilt Top Diagram

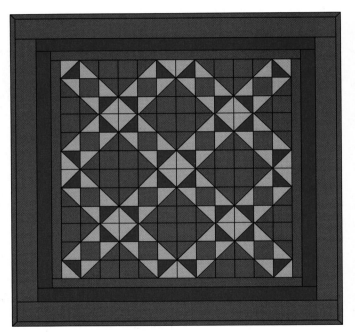

COMPLETING THE QUILT

1 Follow **Quilting**, page 89, to mark, layer, and quilt as desired. Our quilt was machine quilted.

2 Follow **Making Straight Grain Binding**, page 93, to make the binding. For **wall hanging**, make **5¹⁄₈ yds** of 2¹⁄₂" wide binding. For **queen-size** quilt, make **10¹⁄₂ yds** of 2¹⁄₂" wide binding.

3 Follow **Making a Hanging Sleeve**, page 92, to make and attach a hanging sleeve to quilt, if desired.

4 Follow **Attaching Binding with Mitered Corners**, page 93, to attach binding to quilt.

Queen-size Quilt

Dear Quilting Friends,

The patches in the Papa's Plaid quilt were cut from flannel shirts of a friend's grandfather. I made this quilt for her to preserve the memories of her dear "Papa".

In Pieces,

Cindy

Papa's Plaid

Papa's Plaid

Note: *We've included instructions for 2 versions of the wall hanging: the first version uses flannel shirts, purchased fabric, and photo transfers and the second version uses purchased fabric only .*

	Wall Hanging	**Lap-size**
Finished Size	49" x 49" (124 cm x 124 cm)	49" x 63" (124 cm x 160 cm)
Block Size	14" x 14" (36 cm x 36 cm)	14" x 14" (36 cm x 36 cm)
Number of Blocks	9 blocks	12 blocks
Number of Borders	1 border	1 border
Setting	3 x 3 blocks	3 x 4 blocks

YARDAGE

Yardage is based on 45" (114 cm) wide fabric. **Note:** *For flannel shirt version, you will also need photo transfer paper.*

Fabric	**Flannel Shirt Version**
Large Print	Assorted scraps of flannel shirts
White Cotton	1/4 yd (23 cm)
Dark Print	7/8 yd (80cm)
Light Print	7/8 yd (80cm)
Border	1 3/8 yds (1.3 m)
Binding	1/2 yd (46 cm)
Backing	3 1/4 yds (3.0 m)
Batting	57" x 57" (1.5 m x 1.5 m)

Fabric	**Wall Hanging**	**Lap-size**
Large Print	3/4 yd (69 cm)	1 yd (91cm)
Dark Print	7/8 yd (80 cm)	1 yd (91 cm)
Light Print	1 yd (91 cm)	1 1/8 yds (1.0 m)
Border	1 3/8 yds (1.3 m)	1 3/4 yds (1.6 m)
Binding	1/2 yd (46 cm)	1/2 yd (46 cm)
Backing	3 1/4 yds (3.0 m)	4 yds (3.7 m)
Batting	57" x 57" (1.5 m x 1.5 m)	57" x 71" (1.5 m x 1.8 m)

CUTTING OUT THE PIECES

*Follow **Rotary Cutting**, page 87, to cut fabric. All measurements include a 1/4" seam allowance. Cut all strips from the crosswise (selvage to selvage) grain of fabric unless otherwise indicated. Cutting lengths given for borders are exact. You may wish to add an extra 2" of length at each end for "insurance," trimming borders to fit quilt top center.*

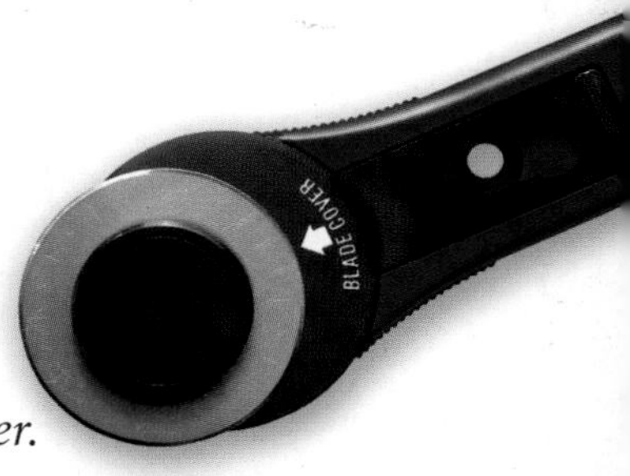

Fabric	Flannel Shirt Version
Flannel Shirt Fabrics	☐ Cut 32 squares (**A1**) 4½" x 4½" and 4 corner squares (**G**) 3½" x 3½".
White Cotton Fabric	☐ Cut 4 squares (**A2**) 6½" x 6½" for photo transfers.
Dark Print	☐ Cut 3 strips (**B**) 2½" wide for Strip Set A. ☐ Cut 2 strips (**C**) 6½" wide for Strip Set C. ☐ Cut 3 strips 2½" wide. From these strips, cut 18 rectangles (**D**) 2½" x 6½".
Light Print	☐ Cut 3 strips (**E**) 4½" wide for Strip Set A. ☐ Cut 1 strip (**F**) 2½" wide for Strip Set C. ☐ Cut 4 strips 2½" wide. From these strips, cut 36 rectangles (**F1**) 2½" x 4½".
Border	☐ Cut 4 lengthwise borders (**H**) 3½" x 42½".
Binding	☐ Cut 6 strips 2½" wide.

Fabric	Wall Hanging	Lap-size
Large Print	☐ Cut 5 strips (**A**) 4½" wide for Strip Set B.	☐ Cut 6 strips (**A**) 4½" wide for Strip Set B.
Dark Print	☐ Cut 3 strips (**B**) 2½" wide for Strip Set A. ☐ Cut 2 strips (**C**) 6½" wide for Strip Set C. ☐ Cut 3 strips 2½" wide. From these strips, cut 18 rectangles (**D**) 2½" x 6½".	☐ Cut 3 strips (**B**) 2½" wide for Strip Set A. ☐ Cut 2 strips (**C**) 6½" wide for Strip Set C. ☐ Cut 4 strips 2½" wide. From these strips, cut 24 rectangles (**D**) 2½" x 6½".
Light Print	☐ Cut 3 strips (**E**) 4½" wide for Strip Set A. ☐ Cut 6 strips (**F**) 2½" wide for Strip Sets B and C. ☐ Cut 1 strip 3½" wide. From this strip, cut 4 corner squares (**G**) 3½" x 3½".	☐ Cut 3 strips (**E**) 4½" wide for Strip Set A. ☐ Cut 7 strips (**F**) 2½" wide for Strip Sets B and C. ☐ Cut 1 strip 3½" wide. From this strip, cut 4 corner squares (**G**) 3½" x 3½".
Border	☐ Cut 4 lengthwise borders (**H**) 3½" x 42½".	☐ Cut 2 lengthwise side borders (**H**) 3½" x 56½". ☐ Cut 2 lengthwise top/bottom borders (**I**) 3½" x 42½".
Binding	☐ Cut 6 strips 2½" wide.	☐ Cut 6 strips 2½" wide.

MAKING THE BLOCKS

Follow **Piecing** *and* **Pressing**, *pages 87-88, to make the blocks. Use a* $1/4$*" seam allowance for all seams.*

1 Sew 1 dark print strip (**B**) and 1 light print strip (**E**) together as shown to make **Strip Set A**. Make 3 **Strip Set A's**. Cut across **Strip Set A's** at $2^1/2$" intervals to make **Unit 1**. For **wall hangings**, make **36 Unit 1's**. For **lap-size** quilt, make **48 Unit 1's**.

2 Sew 1 light print strip (**F**) and 1 large print strip (**A**) together as shown to make **Strip Set B**. For **wall hanging**, make **5 Strip Set B's**. Cut across **Strip Set B's** at $4^1/2$" intervals to make **36 Unit 2's**.
For **lap-size** quilt, make **6 Strip Set B's**. Cut across **Strip Set B's** at $4^1/2$" intervals to make **48 Unit 2's**.
For **flannel shirt** version, follow manufacturer's instructions to transfer photos to cotton squares (**A2**) using photo transfer paper. Trim photo transfer squares to measure $4^1/2$" x $4^1/2$". Sew a light print rectangle (**F1**) to each flannel square (**A1**) and photo transfer square (**A2**) to make **36 Unit 2's**.

3 Sew 1 light print strip (**F**) and 2 dark print strips (**C**) together as shown to make **Strip Set C**. Cut across **Strip Set C** at $2^1/2$" intervals to make **Unit 3**. For **wall hangings**, make **9 Unit 3's**. For **lap-size** quilt, make **12 Unit 3's**.

Strip Set A

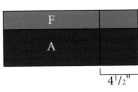

2½"

Unit 1

Strip Set B

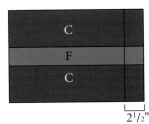

4½"

Unit 2

Strip Set C

2½"

Unit 3

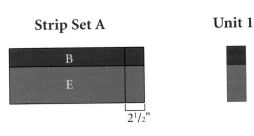

4 Sew 2 **Unit 1's**, 2 **Unit 2's**, and 1 dark print rectangle (**D**) together as shown to make **Unit 4**.
For **flannel shirt** version, make **16 Unit 4's** using shirt fabric and **2 Unit 4's** using photo transfers.
For **wall hanging**, make **18 Unit 4's**.
For **lap-size** quilt, make **24 Unit 4's**.

5 Sew 2 **Unit 4's** and **Unit 3** together as shown to make **Block**.
For **flannel shirt** version, make **8 Blocks** using shirt fabric and **1 Block** using photo transfers.
For **wall hanging**, make **9 Blocks**.
For **lap-size** quilt, make **12 Blocks**.

ASSEMBLING THE QUILT TOP

Refer to **Quilt Top Diagrams**, *page 52, for placement.*

Wall Hanging

1 Sew **3 Blocks** together to make a **Row**.
Make **3 Rows**.

2 Sew **Rows** together to make **Quilt Top Center**.

Lap-size

1 Sew **3 Blocks** together to make a **Row**.
Make **4 Rows**.

2 Sew **Rows** together to make **Quilt Top Center**.

Unit 4

Block Diagram

ADDING THE BORDERS

1 Sew 2 borders (**H**) to sides of **Quilt Top Center**.

2 For **wall hangings**, sew 1 corner square (**G**) to each end of remaining borders (**H**) to make 2 **Border Units**.
For **lap-size** quilt, sew 1 corner square (**G**) to each end of top/bottom borders (**I**) to make 2 **Border Units**.

3 Sew 1 **Border Unit** to top and bottom of pieced center to make **Quilt Top**.

COMPLETING THE QUILT

1 Follow **Quilting**, page 89, to mark, layer, and quilt as desired. Our quilt was machine quilted.

2 Follow **Making Straight Grain Binding**, page 93, to make binding.
For **wall hanging**, make **5⁷/₈ yds** of 2¹/₂" wide binding.
For **lap-size** quilt, make **6⁵/₈ yds** of 2¹/₂" wide binding.

3 Follow **Making a Hanging Sleeve**, page 92, to make and attach a hanging sleeve to quilt, if desired.

4 Follow **Attaching Binding with Mitered Corners**, page 93, to attach binding to quilt.

Wall Hanging Top Diagram

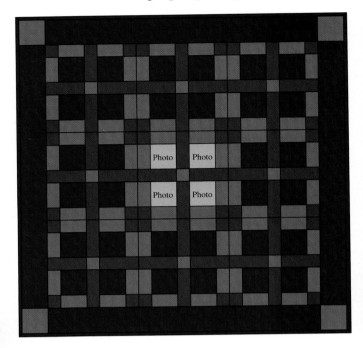

Lap-Size Quilt Top Diagram

Wall Hanging

I sewed a pocket from one of the flannel shirts to the back of the quilt to hold a special poem my friend wrote about her grandfather.

Cindy

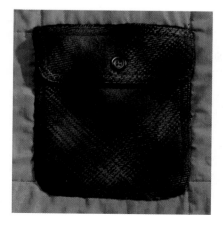

Dear Quilting Friends,

This quilt is very similar to the Prairie Garden quilt. Its stars are created with the addition of flying geese units made with contrasting colors.

In Pieces,

Cindy

Stairway to my Garden

Stairway to my Garden

	Wall Hanging	Queen-size
Finished Size	43" x 43" (109 cm x 109 cm)	89" x 105" (226 cm x 267 cm)
Block Size	16" x 16" (41 cm x 41 cm)	16" x 16" (41 cm x 41 cm)
Number of Blocks	4 blocks	20 blocks
Number Of Borders	2 borders	3 borders
Setting	2 x 2 blocks	4 x 5 blocks

YARDAGE

Yardage is based on 45" (114 cm) wide fabric.

Fabric	Wall Hanging	Queen-size
Large Print	$1/2$ yd (46 cm)	$2^1/8$ yds (1.9 m)
Light Print	$3/4$ yd (69 cm)	$3^1/4$ yds (3.0 m)
Red Print	$3/8$ yd (34 cm)	$1^3/8$ yds (1.3 m)
Blue Print	$3/8$ yd (34 cm)	$1^3/8$ yds (1.3 m)
Inner Border	$1^1/8$ yds (1.0 m)	$2^5/8$ yds (2.4 m)
Middle Border	None	$2^3/4$ yds (2.5 m)
Outer Border	$1^3/8$ yds (1.3 m)	$3^1/8$ yds (2.9 m)
Binding	$1/2$ yd (46 cm)	$7/8$ yd (80 cm)
Backing	$2^7/8$ yds (2.6 m)	$8^1/8$ yds (7.4 m)
Batting	51" x 51" (1.3 m x 1.3 m)	97" x 113" (2.5 m x 2.9 m)

CUTTING OUT THE PIECES

*Follow **Rotary Cutting**, page 87, to cut fabric. All measurements include a $1/4$" seam allowance. Cut all strips from the crosswise (selvage to selvage) grain of fabric unless otherwise indicated. Cutting lengths given for borders are exact. You may wish to add an extra 2" of length at each end for "insurance," trimming borders to fit quilt top center.*

Fabric	Wall Hanging	Queen-size
Large Print	☐ Cut 1 strip (**A**) $4^1/2$" wide for strip sets. ☐ Cut 2 strips $4^1/2$" wide. From these strips, cut 16 corner squares (**B**) $4^1/2$" x $4^1/2$".	☐ Cut 5 strips (**A**) $4^1/2$" wide for strip sets. ☐ Cut 10 strips $4^1/2$" wide. From these strips, cut 80 corner squares (**B**) $4^1/2$" x $4^1/2$".
Light Print	☐ Cut 1 strip (**C**) $4^1/2$" wide for strip sets. ☐ Cut 2 strips $8^1/2$" wide. From these strips, cut 16 rectangles (**D**) $8^1/2$" x $4^1/2$" for flying geese units.	☐ Cut 5 strips (**C**) $4^1/2$" wide for strip sets. ☐ Cut 10 strips $8^1/2$" wide. From these strips, cut 80 rectangles (**D**) $8^1/2$" x $4^1/2$" for flying geese units.
Red Print	☐ Cut 2 strips $4^1/2$" wide. From these strips, cut 16 squares (**E**) $4^1/2$" x $4^1/2$" for flying geese units.	☐ Cut 10 strips $4^1/2$" wide. From these strips, cut 80 squares (**E**) $4^1/2$" x $4^1/2$" for flying geese units.
Blue Print	☐ Cut 2 strips $4^1/2$" wide. From these strips, cut 16 squares (**F**) $4^1/2$" x $4^1/2$" for flying geese units.	☐ Cut 10 strips $4^1/2$" wide. From these strips, cut 80 squares (**F**) $4^1/2$" x $4^1/2$" for flying geese units.
Inner Border	☐ Cut 2 lengthwise top/bottom borders (**G**) 2" x $32^1/2$". ☐ Cut 2 lengthwise side borders (**H**) 2" x $35^1/2$".	☐ Cut 2 lengthwise top/bottom borders (**G**) $3^1/2$" x $64^1/2$". ☐ Cut 2 lengthwise side borders (**H**) $3^1/2$" x $86^1/2$".
Middle Border	None	☐ Cut 2 lengthwise top/bottom borders (**I**) $2^1/2$" x $70^1/2$". ☐ Cut 2 lengthwise side borders (**J**) $2^1/2$" x $90^1/2$".
Outer Border	☐ Cut 2 lengthwise top/bottom borders (**I**) 4" x $35^1/2$". ☐ Cut 2 lengthwise side borders (**J**) 4" x $42^1/2$".	☐ Cut 2 lengthwise top/bottom borders (**K**) $7^1/2$" x $74^1/2$". ☐ Cut 2 lengthwise side borders (**L**) $7^1/2$" x $104^1/2$".
Binding	☐ Cut 5 strips $2^1/2$" wide.	☐ Cut 10 strips $2^1/2$" wide.

MAKING THE BLOCKS

*Follow **Piecing** and **Pressing**, pages 87-88, to make the blocks. Use a ¹/₄" seam allowance for all seams.*

1 Follow **Making Flying Geese**, page 88, using light print rectangles (**D**), blue print squares (**F**), and red print squares (**E**) to make **Unit 1's** and **Unit 2's**.
For **wall hanging**, make **8 Unit 1's** and **8 Unit 2's**.
For **queen-size** quilt, make **40 Unit 1's** and **40 Unit 2's**.

2 Sew 1 large print strip (**A**) and 1 light print strip (**C**) together as shown to make **Strip Set**.
For **wall hanging**, make **1 Strip Set**. Cut across **Strip Set** at 4¹/₂" intervals to make **8 Unit 3's**.
For **queen-size** quilt, make **5 Strip Sets**. Cut across **Strip Sets** at 4¹/₂" intervals to make **40 Unit 3's**.

3 Alternating colors, sew 2 **Unit 3's** together as shown to make **Unit 4**.
For **wall hanging**, make **4 Unit 4's**.
For **queen-size** quilt, make **20 Unit 4's**.

Unit 1

Unit 2

Strip Set

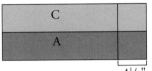

4¹/₂"

Unit 3

Unit 4

4 Sew 2 **Unit 1's** and **Unit 4** together as shown to make **Unit 5**.
For **wall hanging**, make **4 Unit 5's**.
For **queen-size** quilt, make **20 Unit 5's**.

5 Sew 2 large print squares (**B**) and 1 **Unit 2** together as shown to make **Unit 6**.
For **wall hanging**, make **8 Unit 6's**.
For **queen-size** quilt, make **40 Unit 6's**.

6 Sew 2 **Unit 6's** and 1 **Unit 5** together as shown to make **Block**.
For **wall hanging**, make **4 Blocks**.
For **queen-size** quilt, make **20 Blocks**.

ASSEMBLING THE QUILT TOP

*Refer to **Quilt Top Diagrams**, page 60, for placement.*

Wall Hanging

1 Sew **2 Blocks** together as shown to make a **Row**. Make **2 Rows**.

2 Sew **Rows** together to make **Quilt Top Center**.

Queen-size

1 Sew **4 Blocks** together as shown to make a **Row**. Make **5 Rows**.

2 Sew **Rows** together to make **Quilt Top Center**.

Unit 5

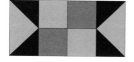

Unit 6

Block Diagram

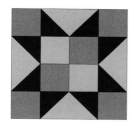

Wall Hanging Row

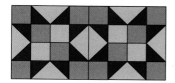

Queen-size Quilt Row

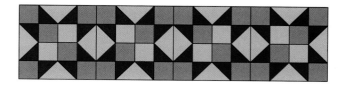

ADDING THE BORDERS

Wall Hanging

1 Sew inner top/bottom borders (**G**), then inner side borders (**H**) to **Quilt Top Center**.

2 Sew outer top/bottom borders (**I**), then outer side borders (**J**) to pieced center to make **Quilt Top**.

Queen-size Quilt

1 Sew inner top/bottom borders (**G**), then inner side borders (**H**) to **Quilt Top Center**.

2 Sew middle top/bottom borders (**I**), then middle side borders (**J**) to pieced center.

3 Sew outer top/bottom borders (**K**), then outer side borders (**L**) to pieced center to make **Quilt Top**.

Wall Hanging Top Diagram

Queen-size Quilt Top Diagram

COMPLETING THE QUILT

1 Follow **Quilting**, page 89, to mark, layer, and quilt as desired. Our quilt was machine quilted.

2 Follow **Making Straight Grain Binding**, page 93, to make the binding.
For **wall hanging**, make **5¹/₈ yds** of 2¹/₂" wide binding.
For **queen-size** quilt, make **11¹/₈ yds** of 2¹/₂" wide binding.

3 Follow **Making a Hanging Sleeve**, page 92, to make and attach a hanging sleeve to quilt, if desired.

4 Follow **Attaching Binding with Mitered Corners**, page 93, to attach binding to quilt.

Queen-size Quilt

Dear Quilting Friends,

This design appears to have sashings and alternate blocks; however, one simple block creates all the additional elements and excitement in this quilt. You can piece a wall hanging with only 1 block or a lap-size quilt with 6 blocks.

In Pieces,

Cindy

Stars and Bars

Stars and Bars

	Wall Hanging	Lap-size
Finished Size	36" x 36" (91 cm x 91 cm)	61" x 81" (155 cm x 206 cm)
Block Size	20" x 20" (51 cm x 51 cm)	20" x 20" (51 cm x 51 cm)
Number of Blocks	1 block	6 blocks
Number Of Borders	2 borders	3 borders
Setting	1 x 1 blocks	2 x 3 blocks

YARDAGE

Yardage is based on 45" (114 cm) wide fabric.

Fabric	Wall Hanging	Lap-size
Large Print	$1/4$ yd (23 cm)	$1/4$ yd (23 cm)
Tan Print	$3/8$ yd (34 cm)	$1^1/8$ yds (1.0 m)
Cream Print	$3/8$ yd (34 cm)	$5/8$ yd (57 cm)
Dark Red Print	$1/4$ yd (23 cm)	$3/4$ yd (69 cm)
Blue Print	$3/8$ yd (34 cm)	$3/4$ yd (69 cm)
Inner Border	$7/8$ yd (80 cm)	$1^7/8$ yds (1.7 m)
Middle Border	None	2 yds (1.8 m)
Outer Border	$1^1/8$ yds (1.0 m)	$2^3/8$ yds (2.2 m)
Binding	$3/8$ yd (34 cm)	$5/8$ yd (57 cm)
Backing	$2^1/2$ yds (2.3 m)	5 yds (4.6 m)
Batting	44" x 44" (1.1 m x 1.1 m)	69" x 89" (1.8 m x 2.3 m)

CUTTING OUT THE PIECES

*Follow **Rotary Cutting**, page 87, to cut fabric. All measurements include a ¹/₄" seam allowance. Cut all fabric from the crosswise (selvage to selvage) grain of fabric unless otherwise indicated. Cutting lengths given for borders are exact. You may wish to add an extra 2" of length at each end for "insurance," trimming borders to fit quilt top center.*

Fabric	Wall Hanging	Lap-size
Large Print	☐ Cut 1 center square (**A**) 5¹/₂" x 5¹/₂".	☐ Cut 1 strip 5¹/₂" wide. From this strip, cut 6 center squares (**A**) 5¹/₂" x 5¹/₂".
Tan Print	☐ Cut 1 strip (**B**) 5¹/₂" wide for strip set. ☐ Cut 1 strip 3" wide. From this strip, cut 4 rectangles (**C**) 3" x 5¹/₂" for flying geese units.	☐ Cut 4 strips (**B**) 5¹/₂" wide for strip sets. ☐ Cut 4 strips 3" wide. From these strips, cut 24 rectangles (**C**) 3" x 5¹/₂" for flying geese units.
Cream Print	☐ Cut 1 strip (**D**) 5⁷/₈" wide for triangle-squares. ☐ Cut 1 strip 3" wide. From this strip, cut 4 squares (**E**) 3" x 3".	☐ Cut 2 strips (**D**) 5⁷/₈" wide for triangle-squares. ☐ Cut 2 strips 3" wide. From these strips, cut 24 squares (**E**) 3" x 3".
Dark Red Print	☐ Cut 2 strips (**F**) 3" wide for strip sets.	☐ Cut 8 strips (**F**) 3" wide for strip sets.
Blue Print	☐ Cut 1 strip (**G**) 5⁷/₈" wide for triangle-squares. ☐ Cut 1 strip 3" wide. From this strip, cut 8 squares (**H**) 3" x 3" for flying geese units.	☐ Cut 2 strips (**G**) 5⁷/₈" wide for triangle-squares. ☐ Cut 4 strips 3" wide. From these strips, cut 48 squares (**H**) 3" x 3" for flying geese units.
Inner Border	☐ Cut 2 lengthwise side borders (**I**) 3" x 20¹/₂". ☐ Cut 2 lengthwise top/bottom borders (**J**) 3" x 25¹/₂".	☐ Cut 2 lengthwise side borders (**I**) 3" x 60¹/₂". ☐ Cut 2 lengthwise top/bottom borders (**J**) 3" x 45¹/₂".
Middle Border	None	☐ Cut 2 lengthwise side borders (**K**) 5¹/₂" x 65¹/₂". ☐ Cut 2 lengthwise top/bottom borders (**L**) 5¹/₂" x 55¹/₂".
Outer Border	☐ Cut 2 lengthwise side borders (**K**) 5¹/₂" x 25¹/₂". ☐ Cut 2 lengthwise top/bottom borders (**L**) 5¹/₂" x 35¹/₂".	☐ Cut 2 lengthwise side borders (**M**) 3" x 75¹/₂". ☐ Cut 2 lengthwise top/bottom borders (**N**) 3" x 60¹/₂".
Binding	☐ Cut 4 strips 2¹/₂" wide.	☐ Cut 8 strips 2¹/₂" wide.

MAKING THE BLOCKS

*Follow **Piecing** and **Pressing**, pages 87-88, to make the blocks. Use a ¼" seam allowance for all seams.*

1 Follow **Making Flying Geese**, page 88, using tan print rectangles (**C**) and blue print squares (**H**) to make **Unit 1**.
For **wall hanging**, make **4 Unit 1's**.
For **lap-size** quilt, make **24 Unit 1's**.

2 Sew 2 **Unit 1's** and center square (**A**) together as shown to make **Unit 2**.
For **wall hanging**, make **1 Unit 2**.
For **lap-size** quilt, make **6 Unit 2's**.

3 Sew 2 cream squares (**E**) and **Unit 1** together as shown to make **Unit 3**.
For **wall hanging**, make **2 Unit 3's**.
For **lap-size** quilt, make **12 Unit 3's**.

4 Sew 2 **Unit 3's** and 1 **Unit 2** together as shown to make **Unit 4**.

Unit 1

Unit 2

Unit 3

Unit 4

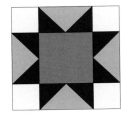

5 Sew 1 tan print strip (**B**) and 2 dark red print strips (**F**) together as shown to make **Strip Set**.
For **wall hanging**, make **1 Strip Set**. Cut across **Strip Set** at 5½" intervals to make **4 Unit 5's**.
For **lap-size** quilt, make **4 Strip Sets**. Cut across **Strip Sets** at 5½" intervals to make **24 Unit 5's**.

6 Matching right sides and raw edges, stack a cream print strip (**D**) on a blue print strip (**G**) as shown in **Fig. 1**.
For **wall hanging**, make **1** layered strip. Cut layered strip at 5⅞" intervals to make **2 Unit 6** layered squares. Do not separate squares.
For **lap-size** quilt, make **2** layered strips. Cut layered strips at 5⅞" intervals to make **12 Unit 6** layered squares. Do not separate squares.

7 Draw a diagonal line (corner to corner) on wrong side of each cream print **Unit 6** square. Stitch seam ¼" from each side of drawn line (**Fig. 2**). Trim along drawn line and press open to make 2 **Unit 7** triangle-squares.
For **wall hanging**, make **4 Unit 7's**.
For **lap-size** quilt, make **24 Unit 7's**.

8 Sew 2 **Unit 7's** and 1 **Unit 5** together as shown to make **Unit 8**.
For **wall hanging**, make **2 Unit 8's**.
For **lap-size** quilt, make **12 Unit 8's**.

9 Sew 2 **Unit 5's** and 1 **Unit 4** together as shown to make **Unit 9**.
For **wall hanging**, make **1 Unit 9**.
For **lap-size** quilt, make **6 Unit 9's**.

10 Sew 2 **Unit 8's** and 1 **Unit 9** together as shown to make **Block**.
For **wall hanging**, make **1 Block**.
For **lap-size** quilt, make **6 Blocks**.

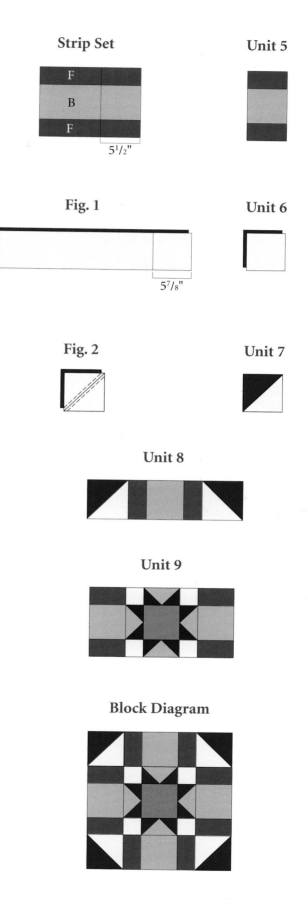

Strip Set

Unit 5

Fig. 1

Unit 6

5⅞"

Fig. 2

Unit 7

Unit 8

Unit 9

Block Diagram

ASSEMBLING THE QUILT TOP

*Refer to **Quilt Top Diagrams** for placement.*

Lap-size Quilt

1 Sew **2 Blocks** together as shown to make a **Row**. Make **3 Rows**.

2 Sew **Rows** together to make **Quilt Top Center**.

ADDING THE BORDERS

Wall Hanging

1 Sew inner side borders (**I**), then inner top/bottom borders (**J**) to **Block**.

2 Sew outer side borders (**K**), then outer top/bottom borders (**L**) to pieced center to make **Quilt Top**.

Lap-size Quilt

1 Sew inner side borders (**I**), then inner top/bottom borders (**J**) to **Quilt Top Center**.

2 Sew middle side borders (**K**), then middle top/bottom borders (**L**) to pieced center.

3 Sew outer side borders (**M**), then outer top/bottom borders (**N**) to pieced center to make **Quilt Top**.

Wall Hanging Top Diagram

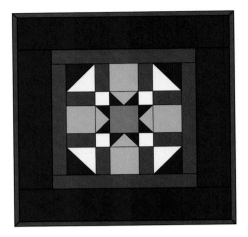

Lap-size Quilt Top Diagram

COMPLETING THE QUILT

1. Follow **Quilting**, page 89, to mark, layer, and quilt as desired. Our quilt was machine quilted.

2. Follow **Making Straight Grain Binding**, page 93, to make binding.
For **wall hanging**, make **4³⁄₈ yds** of 2¹⁄₂" wide binding.
For **lap-size** quilt, make **8¹⁄₄ yds** of 2¹⁄₂" wide binding.

3. Follow **Making a Hanging Sleeve**, page 92, to make and attach a hanging sleeve to quilt, if desired.

4. Follow **Attaching Binding with Mitered Corners**, page 93, to attach binding to quilt.

Lap-size Quilt

Dear Quilting Friends,

This design only requires 12 blocks to make a full-size quilt. Four blocks will make a matching wall hanging. The color placement in the corner triangles creates the stars.

In Pieces,

Fancy's Star

Fancy's Star

	Wall Hanging	Full-size
Finished Size	53" x 53" (135 cm x 135 cm)	82" x 100" (208 cm x 254 cm)
Block Size	18" x 18" (46 cm x 46 cm)	18" x 18" (46 cm x 46 cm)
Number of Blocks	4 blocks	12 blocks
Number Of Borders	2 borders	2 borders
Setting	2 x 2 blocks	3 x 4 blocks

YARDAGE

Yardage is based on 45" (114 cm) wide fabric.

Fabric	Wall Hanging	Full-size
Large Print	$1/2$ yd (46 cm)	$1 1/8$ yds (1.0 m)
Green Print	$3/8$ yd (34 cm)	$3/4$ yd (69 m)
Cream Print	$1 1/4$ yds (1.1 m)	3 yds (2.7 m)
Dark Red Print	$5/8$ yd (57 cm)	$1 3/4$ yds (1.6 m)
Inner Border	$1 1/4$ yds (1.1 m)	$2 1/4$ yds (2.1 m)
Outer Border	$1 5/8$ yds (1.5 m)	$2 1/2$ yds (2.3 m)
Binding	$1/2$ yd (46 cm)	$7/8$ yd (80 cm)
Backing	$3 1/2$ yds (3.2 m)	$7 1/2$ yds (6.9 m)
Batting	61" x 61" (1.5 m x 1.5 m)	90" x 108" (2.3 m x 2.7 m)

CUTTING OUT THE PIECES

*Follow **Rotary Cutting**, page 87, to cut fabric. All measurements include a $^1/_4$" seam allowance. Cut all fabric from the crosswise (selvage to selvage) grain of fabric unless otherwise indicated. Cutting lengths given for borders are exact. You may wish to add an extra 2" of length at each end for "insurance," trimming borders to fit quilt top center.*

Fabric	Wall Hanging	Full-size
Large Print	☐ Cut 1 strip $6^7/_8$" wide. From this strip, cut 2 squares $6^7/_8$" x $6^7/_8$". Cut each square once diagonally to make 4 triangles (**A**). ☐ Cut 1 strip $6^1/_2$" wide. From this strip, cut 4 center squares (**B**) $6^1/_2$" x $6^1/_2$".	☐ Cut 3 strips $6^7/_8$" wide. From these strips, cut 12 squares $6^7/_8$" x $6^7/_8$". Cut each square once diagonally to make 24 triangles (**A**). ☐ Cut 2 strips $6^1/_2$" wide. From these strips, cut 12 center squares (**B**) $6^1/_2$" x $6^1/_2$".
Green Print	☐ Cut 2 strips $5^1/_8$" wide. From these strips, cut 8 squares $5^1/_8$" x $5^1/_8$". Cut each square once diagonally to make 16 triangles (**C**).	☐ Cut 4 strips $5^1/_8$" wide. From these strips, cut 24 squares $5^1/_8$" x $5^1/_8$". Cut each square once diagonally to make 48 triangles (**C**).
Cream Print	☐ Cut 2 strips 9" wide. From these strips, cut 16 rectangles (**D**) 9" x $4^3/_4$" for flying geese units. ☐ Cut 1 strip $7^1/_4$" wide. From this strip, cut 4 squares $7^1/_4$" x $7^1/_4$". Cut each square twice diagonally to make 16 triangles (**E**). ☐ Cut 2 strips $6^7/_8$" wide. From these strips, cut 6 squares $6^7/_8$" x $6^7/_8$". Cut each square once diagonally to make 12 triangles (**F**).	☐ Cut 6 strips 9" wide. From these strips, cut 48 rectangles (**D**) 9" x $4^3/_4$" for flying geese units. ☐ Cut 3 strips $7^1/_4$" wide. From these strips, cut 12 squares $7^1/_4$" x $7^1/_4$". Cut each square twice diagonally to make 48 triangles (**E**). ☐ Cut 3 strips $6^7/_8$" wide. From these strips, cut 12 squares $6^7/_8$" x $6^7/_8$". Cut each square once diagonally to make 24 triangles (**F**).
Dark Red Print	☐ Cut 4 strips $4^3/_4$" wide. From these strips, cut 32 squares (**G**) $4^3/_4$" x $4^3/_4$".	☐ Cut 12 strips $4^3/_4$" wide. From these strips, cut 96 squares (**G**) $4^3/_4$" x $4^3/_4$".
Inner Border	☐ Cut 2 lengthwise side borders (**H**) $2^1/_2$" x $36^1/_2$". ☐ Cut 2 lengthwise top/bottom borders (**I**) $2^1/_2$" x $40^1/_2$".	☐ Cut 2 lengthwise side borders (**H**) 4" x $72^1/_2$". ☐ Cut 2 lengthwise top/bottom borders (**I**) 4" x $61^1/_2$".
Outer Border	☐ Cut 2 lengthwise side borders (**J**) $6^1/_2$" x $40^1/_2$". ☐ Cut 2 lengthwise top/bottom borders (**K**) $6^1/_2$" x $52^1/_2$".	☐ Cut 2 lengthwise side borders (**J**) $10^1/_2$" x $79^1/_2$". ☐ Cut 2 lengthwise top/bottom borders (**K**) $10^1/_2$" x $81^1/_2$".
Binding	☐ Cut 6 strips $2^1/_2$" wide.	☐ Cut 10 strips $2^1/_2$" wide.

MAKING THE BLOCKS

*Follow **Piecing** and **Pressing**, pages 87-88, to make the blocks. Use a ¼" seam allowance for all seams.*

1 Matching centers, sew 4 green triangles (**C**) and large print square (**B**) together as shown to make **Unit 1**.
For **wall hanging**, make **4 Unit 1's**.
For **full-size** quilt, make **12 Unit 1's**.

2 Follow **Making Flying Geese**, page 88, using cream print rectangles (**D**) and dark red print squares (**G**) to make **Unit 2**.
For **wall hanging**, make **16 Unit 2's**.
For **full-size** quilt, make **48 Unit 2's**.

3 Sew 2 cream print triangles (**E**) and 1 **Unit 2** together as shown to make **Unit 3**.
For **wall hanging**, make **8 Unit 3's**.
For **full-size** quilt, make **24 Unit 3's**.

4 Sew 2 **Unit 2's** and **Unit 1** together as shown to make **Unit 4**.
For **wall hanging**, make **4 Unit 4's**.
For **full-size** quilt, make **12 Unit 4's**.

5 Sew 2 **Unit 3's** and **Unit 4** together as shown to make **Unit 5**.
For **wall hanging**, make **4 Unit 5's**.
For **full-size** quilt, make **12 Unit 5's**.

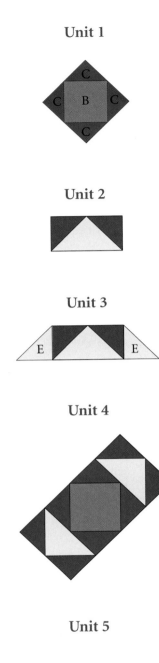

Unit 1

Unit 2

Unit 3

Unit 4

Unit 5

6 For **wall hanging** and **full-size** quilts, sew 3 cream print triangles (**F**) and 1 large print triangle (**A**) to each of 4 **Unit 5's** as shown to make **4 Block A's**.

7 For **full-size** quilt only, sew 2 cream print triangles (**F**) and 2 large print triangles (**A**) to each of 6 **Unit 5's** as shown to make **6 Block B's**.

8 For **full-size** quilt only, sew 4 large print triangles (**A**) to each of 2 **Unit 5's** as shown to make **2 Block C's**.

ASSEMBLING THE QUILT TOP

*Refer to **Quilt Top Diagrams**, page 76, for placement.*

Wall Hanging

1 Sew **2 Block A's** together as shown to make a **Row**. Make **2 Rows**.

2 Sew **Rows** together to make **Quilt Top Center**.

Full-size Quilt

1 Sew **2 Block A's** and **1 Block B** together as shown to make **Row 1**. Make **2 Row 1's**.

2 Sew **2 Block B's** and **1 Block C** together as shown to make **Row 2**. Make **2 Row 2's**.

3 Sew **Rows 1** and **2** together as shown to make **Quilt Top Center**.

Block A Diagram

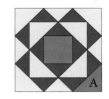

Block B Diagram

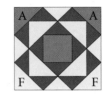

Block C Diagram

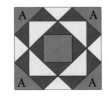

Wall Hanging Row (make 2)

Full-size Row 1 (make 2)

Row 2 (make 2)

ADDING THE BORDERS

Wall Hanging

1 Sew inner side borders (**H**), then inner top/bottom borders (**I**) to **Quilt Top Center**.

2 Sew outer side borders (**J**), then outer top/bottom borders (**K**) to pieced center to make **Quilt Top**.

Full-size Quilt

1 Sew inner side borders (**H**), then inner top/bottom borders (**I**) to **Quilt Top Center**.

2 Sew outer side borders (**J**), then outer top/bottom borders (**K**) to pieced center to make **Quilt Top**.

COMPLETING THE QUILT

1 Follow **Quilting**, page 89, to mark, layer, and quilt as desired. Our quilt was machine quilted.

2 Follow **Making Straight Grain Binding**, page 93, to make binding.
For **wall hanging**, make **6¼ yds** of 2½" wide binding.
For **full-size** quilt, make **10½ yds** of 2½" wide binding.

3 Follow **Making a Hanging Sleeve**, page 92, to make and attach a hanging sleeve to quilt, if desired.

4 Follow **Attaching Binding with Mitered Corners**, page 93, to attach binding to quilt.

Wall Hanging Top Diagram

Full-size Quilt Top Diagram

Dear Quilting Friends,

Pick 3 inspiration fabrics for this quilt — a medium and large floral print with very little background showing for the blocks and a large-scale open floral with a lot of background color showing for the border. Make either a twin or full-size quilt with just 12 blocks by varying the number and size of the borders.

In Pieces,

Cindy

Flower Patch

Flower Patch

	Twin-size	Full-size
Finished Size	69$\frac{1}{4}$" x 89" (176 cm x 226 cm)	84$\frac{1}{4}$" x 104" (214 cm x 264 cm)
Block Size	14" x 14" (36 cm x 36 cm)	14" x 14" (36 cm x 36 cm)
Number of Blocks	12 blocks	12 blocks
Number Of Borders	1 border	2 borders
Setting	3 x 4 blocks on point	3 x 4 blocks on point

YARDAGE

Yardage is based on 45" (114 cm) wide fabric.

Fabric	Twin-size	Full-size
Light Floral Print	1$\frac{3}{8}$ yds (1.3 m)	1$\frac{3}{8}$ yds (1.3 m)
Dark Floral Print	3 yds (2.7 m)	3 yds (2.7 m)
Red Print	$\frac{3}{4}$ yd (69 cm)	$\frac{7}{8}$ yd (80 cm)
Gold Print	1$\frac{1}{2}$ yds (1.4 m)	1$\frac{1}{2}$ yds (1.4 m)
Inner Border	None	2$\frac{1}{2}$ yds (2.3 m)
Outer Border	2$\frac{1}{2}$ yds (2.3 m)	2$\frac{3}{4}$ yds (2.5 m)
Binding	$\frac{3}{4}$ yd (69 cm)	$\frac{7}{8}$ yd (80 cm)
Backing	5$\frac{1}{2}$ yds (5.0 m)	7$\frac{3}{4}$ yds (7.1 m)
Batting	77" x 97" (2.0 m x 2.5 m)	92" x 112" (2.3 m x 2.8 m)

CUTTING OUT THE PIECES

*Follow **Rotary Cutting**, page 87, to cut fabric. All measurements include a $1/4$" seam allowance. Cut all fabric from the crosswise (selvage to selvage) grain of fabric unless otherwise indicated. Cutting lengths given for borders are exact. You may wish to add an extra 2" of length at each end for "insurance," trimming borders to fit quilt top center.*

Fabric	Twin-size	Full-size
Light Floral Print	☐ Cut 3 strips $14^1/2$" wide. From these strips, cut 6 squares (**A**) $14^1/2$" x $14^1/2$".	☐ Cut 3 strips $14^1/2$" wide. From these strips, cut 6 squares (**A**) $14^1/2$" x $14^1/2$".
Dark Floral Print	☐ Cut 3 strips (**B**) $7^1/2$" wide for Strip Set A. ☐ Cut 1 strip $10^3/4$" wide. From this strip, cut 2 squares $10^3/4$" x $10^3/4$". Cut each square once diagonally to make 4 corner setting triangles (**C**). ☐ Cut 3 strips 21" wide. From these strips, cut 3 squares 21" x 21". Cut each square twice diagonally to make 12 setting triangles (**D**). Discard 2.	☐ Cut 3 strips (**B**) $7^1/2$" wide for Strip Set A. ☐ Cut 1 strip $10^3/4$" wide. From this strip, cut 2 squares $10^3/4$" x $10^3/4$". Cut each square once diagonally to make 4 corner setting triangles (**C**). ☐ Cut 3 strips 21" wide. From these strips, cut 3 squares 21" x 21". Cut each square twice diagonally to make 12 setting triangles (**D**). Discard 2.
Red Print	☐ Cut 6 strips (**E**) 4" wide for Strip Set B.	☐ Cut 6 strips (**E**) 4" wide for Strip Set B. ☐ Cut 1 strip 4" wide. From this strip, cut 4 corner squares (**J**) 4" x 4" for inner border.
Gold Print	☐ Cut 6 strips (**F**) 4" wide for Strip Set A. ☐ Cut 3 strips (**G**) $7^1/2$" wide for Strip Set B.	☐ Cut 6 strips (**F**) 4" wide for Strip Set A. ☐ Cut 3 strips (**G**) $7^1/2$" wide for Strip Set B.
Inner Border	None	☐ Cut 2 lengthwise inner side borders (**H**) 4" x $79^1/2$". ☐ Cut 2 lengthwise inner top/bottom borders (**I**) 4" x $59^3/4$".
Outer Border	☐ Cut 2 lengthwise outer side borders (**K**) 5" x $79^1/2$". ☐ Cut 2 lengthwise outer top/bottom borders (**L**) 5" x $68^3/4$".	☐ Cut 2 lengthwise outer side borders (**K**) 9" x $86^1/2$". ☐ Cut 2 lengthwise outer top/bottom borders (**L**) 9" x $83^3/4$".
Binding	☐ Cut 9 strips $2^1/2$" wide.	☐ Cut 10 strips $2^1/2$" wide.

MAKING THE BLOCKS

Follow **Piecing** *and* **Pressing**, *pages 87-88, to make the blocks.*

1 Sew 1 dark floral print strip (**B**) and 2 gold print strips (**F**) together as shown to make **Strip Set A**. Make 3 **Strip Set A's**. Cut across **Strip Set A's** at 7¹/₂" intervals to make **Unit 1**. Make 12 **Unit 1's**.

2 Sew 1 gold print strip (**G**) and 2 red print strips (**E**) together as shown to make **Strip Set B**. Make 3 **Strip Set B's**. Cut across **Strip Set B's** at 4" intervals to make **Unit 2**. Make 24 **Unit 2's**.

3 Sew 1 **Unit 1** and 2 **Unit 2's** together as shown to make **Block**. Make 12 **Blocks**.

Strip Set A (make 3)

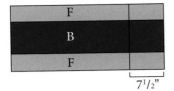

7¹/₂"

Unit 1 (make 12)

Strip Set B (make 3)

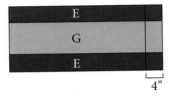

4"

Unit 2 (make 24)

Block Diagram (make 12)

ASSEMBLING THE QUILT TOP

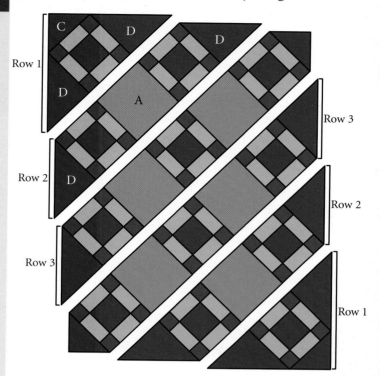

Quilt Top Center Assembly Diagram

*Refer to **Quilt Top Center Assembly Diagram** for placement.*

1 Sew 1 **Block**, 1 corner setting triangle (**C**), and 2 setting triangles (**D**) together as shown to make **Row 1**. Make 2 **Row 1's**.

2 Sew 2 **Blocks**, 1 light floral square (**A**), and 2 setting triangles (**D**) together as shown to make **Row 2**. Make 2 **Row 2's**.

3 Sew 3 **Blocks**, 2 light floral squares (**A**), 1 setting triangle (**D**), and 1 corner setting triangle (**C**) together as shown to make **Row 3**. Make 2 **Row 3's**.

4 Sew **Rows 1, 2**, and **3** together to make **Quilt Top Center**.

ADDING THE BORDERS

*Refer to **Quilt Top Diagrams** for placement.*

Twin-size

1 Sew 2 outer side borders (**K**), then 2 outer top/bottom borders (**L**) to **Quilt Top Center** to make **Quilt Top.**

Full-size

1 Sew 2 inner side borders (**H**) to **Quilt Top Center**.

2 Sew a corner square (**J**) to each end of inner top/bottom borders (**I**) to make 2 **Border Units.**

3 Sew a **Border Unit** to top and bottom of pieced center.

4 Sew 2 outer side borders (**K**), then 2 outer top/bottom borders (**L**) to pieced center to make **Quilt Top.**

Twin-size Quilt Top Diagram

Full-size Quilt Top Diagram

COMPLETING THE QUILT

1 Follow **Quilting**, page 89, to mark, layer, and quilt as desired. Our quilt was machine quilted.

2 Follow **Making Straight Grain Binding**, page 93, to make binding. For **twin-size** quilt, make **9¼ yds** of 2½" wide binding.

For **full-size** quilt, make **10⅞ yds** of 2½" wide binding.

3 Follow **Attaching Binding with Mitered Corners**, page 93, to attach binding to quilt.

Full-size Quilt

General Instructions

To make your quilting easier and more enjoyable, we encourage you to carefully read all of the general instructions, study the color photographs, and familiarize yourself with the individual project instructions before beginning a project.

FABRICS

SELECTING FABRICS

Choose high-quality, medium-weight 100% cotton fabrics. All-cotton fabrics hold a crease better, fray less, and are easier to quilt than cotton/polyester blends.

Yardage requirements listed for each project are based on 45" wide fabric with a "usable" width of 40" after shrinkage and trimming selvages. Actual usable width will probably vary slightly from fabric to fabric. Our recommended yardage lengths should be adequate for occasional re-squaring of fabric when many cuts are required.

PREPARING FABRICS

We recommend that all fabrics be washed, dried, and pressed before cutting. If fabrics are not pre-washed, washing the finished quilt will cause shrinkage and give it a more "antiqued" look and feel. Bright and dark colors, which may run, should always be washed before cutting. After washing and drying fabric, fold lengthwise with wrong sides together and matching selvages.

ROTARY CUTTING

Rotary cutting has brought speed and accuracy to quiltmaking by allowing quilters to easily cut strips of fabric and then cut those strips into smaller pieces.

- Place fabric on work surface with fold closest to you.

- Cut all strips from the selvage-to-selvage width of the fabric unless otherwise indicated in project instructions.

- Square left edge of fabric using rotary cutter and rulers (**Figs. 1-2**).

- To cut each strip required for a project, place ruler over cut edge of fabric, aligning desired marking on ruler with cut edge; make cut (**Fig. 3**).

- When cutting several strips from a single piece of fabric, it is important to make sure that cuts remain at a perfect right angle to the fold; square fabric as needed.

PIECING

Precise cutting, followed by accurate piecing, will ensure that all pieces of the quilt top fit together well.

MACHINE PIECING

- Set sewing machine stitch length for approximately 11 stitches per inch.

- Use neutral-colored general-purpose sewing thread (not quilting thread) in needle and in bobbin.

- An accurate $1/4$" seam allowance is **essential**. Presser feet that are $1/4$" wide are available for most sewing machines.

Fig. 1

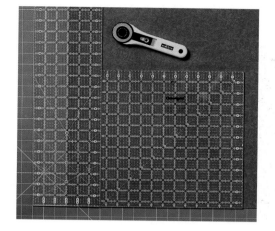

Fig. 2

Fig. 3

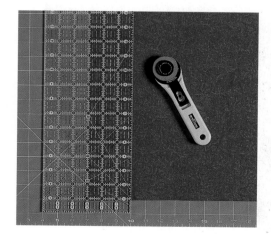

- When piecing, always place pieces right sides together and match raw edges; pin if necessary.

- Chain piecing saves time and will usually result in more accurate piecing.

- Trim away points of seam allowances that extend beyond edges of sewn pieces.

Sewing Strip Sets

When there are several strips to assemble into a strip set, first sew strips together into pairs, then sew pairs together to form strip set. To help avoid distortion, sew seams in opposite directions (**Fig. 4**).

Sewing Across Seam Intersections

When sewing across intersection of 2 seams, place pieces right sides together and match seams exactly, making sure seam allowances are pressed in opposite directions (**Fig. 5**).

Sewing Sharp Points

To ensure sharp points when joining triangular or diagonal pieces, stitch across the center of the "X" (shown in pink) formed on wrong side by previous seams (**Fig. 6**).

Making Flying Geese

1 Place 1 square on 1 end of rectangle and stitch diagonally (**Fig. 7**). Trim ¼" from stitching line (**Fig. 8**). Open up and press, pressing seam allowances to darker fabric (**Fig. 9**).

2 Place another square on opposite end of rectangle. Stitch and trim as shown in **Fig. 10**. Open up and press to complete unit (**Fig. 11**).

PRESSING

- Use steam iron set on "Cotton" for all pressing.

- Press after sewing each seam.

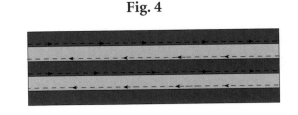

Fig. 4

Fig. 5

Fig. 6

Fig. 7

Fig. 8

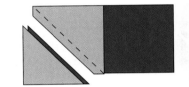

Fig. 9

Fig. 10

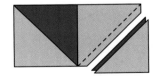

Fig. 11

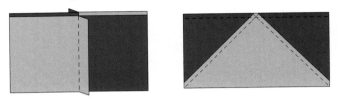

- Seam allowances are almost always pressed to 1 side, usually toward darker fabric. However, to reduce bulk it may occasionally be necessary to press seam allowances toward the lighter fabric or even to press them open.

- To prevent dark fabric seam allowance from showing through light fabric, trim darker seam allowance slightly narrower than lighter seam allowance.

- To press long seams, such as those in long strip sets, without curving or other distortion, lay strips across width of the ironing board.

QUILTING

Quilting holds the 3 layers (top, batting, and backing) of the quilt together and can be done by hand or machine. Because marking, layering, and quilting are interrelated and may be done in different orders depending on circumstances, please read entire **Quilting** *section before beginning project.*

TYPES OF QUILTING DESIGNS

Meandering Quilting
Quilting in random curved lines and swirls is called "meandering" quilting (**Fig. 12**). Quilting lines should not cross or touch each other. This type of quilting does not need to be marked.

In the Ditch Quilting
Quilting along seamlines is called "in the ditch" quilting (**Fig. 13**). This type of quilting should be done on the side **opposite** the seam allowance and does not have to be marked.

Motif Quilting
Quilting a design, such as a feathered wreath, is called "motif" quilting (**Fig. 14**). This type of quilting should be marked before basting quilt layers together.

Fig. 12

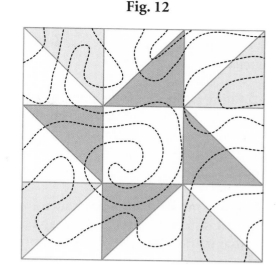

Fig. 13

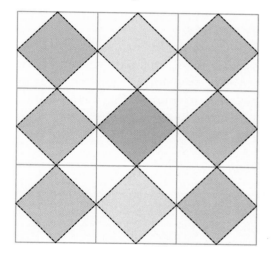

Fig. 14

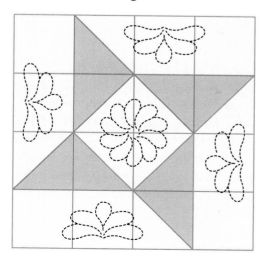

MARKING QUILTING LINES

Quilting lines may be marked using fabric marking pencils, chalk markers, water or air soluble pens, or lead pencils.

Simple quilting designs may be marked with chalk or chalk pencil after basting. A small area may be marked, then quilted, before moving to next area to be marked. Intricate designs should be marked before basting using a more durable marker.

Caution: Some marks may be permanently set by pressing. **Test** different markers **on scrap fabric** to find one that marks clearly and can be thoroughly removed.

A wide variety of pre-cut quilting stencils, as well as entire books of quilting patterns, are available. Using a stencil makes it easier to mark intricate or repetitive designs.

To make a stencil from a pattern, center template plastic over pattern and use a permanent marker to trace pattern onto plastic. Use a craft knife with single or double blade to cut channels along traced lines (**Fig. 15**).

Fig. 15

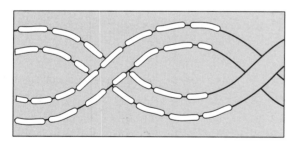

BACKING
PREPARING THE BACKING

To allow for slight shifting of the quilt top during quilting, backing should be approximately 4" larger on all sides. Yardage requirements listed for quilt backings are calculated for 45"w fabric with a "usable width" of 40". Using 90"w or 108"w fabric for the backing of a bed-sized quilt may eliminate piecing. To piece a backing using 45"w fabric, use the following instructions.

1 Measure length and width of quilt top; add 8" to each measurement.

2 If determined width is 80" or less, cut backing fabric into 2 lengths slightly longer than determined **length** measurement. Trim selvages. Place lengths with right sides facing and sew long edges together, forming tube (**Fig. 16**). Match seams and press along 1 fold (**Fig. 17**). Cut along pressed fold to form single piece (**Fig. 18**).

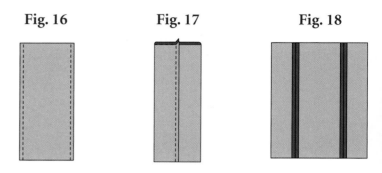

| Fig. 16 | Fig. 17 | Fig. 18 |

3 If determined width is more than 80" it may require less fabric yardage if the backing is pieced horizontally. Divide detemined **length** measurement by 40" to determine how many widths will be needed. Cut required number of widths the determined **width** measurement. Trim selvages. Sew long edges together to form single piece.

4 Trim backing to size determined in Step 1; press seam allowances open.

BATTING
CHOOSING THE BATTING

The appropriate batting will make quilting easier. For fine hand quilting, choose low-loft batting. All cotton or cotton/polyester blend battings work well for machine quilting because the cotton helps "grip" quilt layers. If quilt is to be tied, a high-loft batting, sometimes called extra-loft or fat batting, may be used to make the quilt "fluffy."

Types of batting include cotton, polyester, cotton/polyester blend, wool, cotton/wool blend, and silk.

When selecting batting, refer to package labels for characteristics and care instructions. Cut batting same size as prepared backing.

ASSEMBLING THE QUILT

1 Examine wrong side of quilt top closely; trim any seam allowances and clip any threads that may show through front of the quilt. Press quilt top, being careful not to "set" any marked quilting lines.

2 Place backing **wrong** side up on flat surface. Use masking tape to tape edges of backing to surface. Place batting on top of backing fabric. Smooth batting gently, being careful not to stretch or tear. Center quilt top **right** side up on batting.

3 If machine quilting, use 1" rustproof safety pins to "pin-baste" all layers together, spacing pins approximately 4" apart. Begin at center and work toward outer edges to secure all layers. If possible, place pins away from areas that will be quilted, although pins may be removed as needed when quilting.

Fig. 19

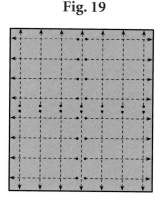

MACHINE QUILTING METHODS

Use general-purpose thread in bobbin. Do not use quilting thread. Thread the needle of machine with general-purpose thread or transparent monofilament thread to make quilting blend with quilt top fabrics. Use decorative thread, such as a metallic or contrasting-color general-purpose thread, to make quilting lines stand out more.

Straight Line Quilting
The term "straight-line" is somewhat deceptive, since curves (especially gentle ones) as well as straight lines can be stitched with this technique.

1 Set stitch length for 6 - 10 stitches per inch and attach walking foot to sewing machine.

2 Determine which section of the quilt will have the longest continuous quilting line, oftentimes the area from center top to center bottom. Roll up and secure each edge of quilt to help reduce the bulk, keeping fabrics smooth. Smaller projects may not need to be rolled.

3 Begin stitching on longest quilting line, using very short stitches for the first $1/4$" to "lock" quilting. Stitch across project, using 1 hand on each side of walking foot to slightly spread fabric and to guide fabric through machine. Lock stitches at end of quilting line.

4 Continue machine quilting, stitching longer quilting lines first to stabilize the quilt before moving on to other areas.

Free Motion Quilting
Free motion quilting may be free form or may follow a marked pattern.

1 Attach darning foot to sewing machine and lower or cover feed dogs.

2 Position quilt under darning foot. Lower presser foot. Holding top thread, take 1 stitch and pull bobbin thread to top of quilt. To "lock" beginning of quilting line, hold top and bobbin threads while making 3 to 5 stitches in place.

3 Use 1 hand on each side of darning foot to slightly spread fabric and to move fabric through the machine. Even stitch length is achieved by using smooth, flowing hand motion and steady machine speed. Slow machine speed and fast hand movement will create long stitches. Fast machine speed and slow hand movement will create short stitches. Move quilt sideways, back and forth, in a circular motion, or in a random motion to create desired designs; do not rotate quilt. Lock stitches at end of each quilting line.

MAKING A HANGING SLEEVE

Attaching a hanging sleeve to the back of a wall hanging or quilt before the binding is added allows the project to be displayed on a wall.

1 Measure width of quilt top edge and subtract 1". Cut piece of fabric 7"w by determined measurement.

2 Press short edges of fabric piece ¼" to wrong side; press edges ¼" to wrong side again and machine stitch in place.

3 Matching wrong sides, fold piece in half lengthwise to form tube.

4 Follow project instructions to trim backing and batting. Before stitching binding to backing, match raw edges and stitch hanging sleeve to center top edge on back of quilt. Sew binding to quilt top.

5 Finish binding quilt, treating hanging sleeve as part of backing.

6 Blindstitch bottom of hanging sleeve to backing, taking care not to stitch through to front of quilt.

7 Insert dowel or slat into hanging sleeve.

BINDING

Binding encloses the raw edges of the quilt and may be cut from the straight crosswise grain of the fabric.

MAKING STRAIGHT-GRAIN BINDING

1 Cut crosswise 2¹/₂" wide strips of binding fabric the determined length called for in the project instructions. Piece strips to achieve the necessary length.

2 Matching wrong sides and raw edges, press strip(s) in half lengthwise to complete binding.

ATTACHING BINDING WITH MITERED CORNERS

1 Trim batting and backing even with quilt top edges. Baste all 3 layers together ¹/₄" from outer edges of the quilt.

2 Beginning with 1 end near center on bottom edge of quilt, lay binding around quilt to make sure that seams in binding will not end up at a corner. Adjust placement if necessary. Matching raw edges of binding to raw edge of quilt back, pin binding to quilt back along 1 edge.

3 When you reach first corner, mark ¹/₄" from corner of quilt back (**Fig. 20**).

4 Beginning 4" from end of binding and using ¹/₄" seam allowance, sew binding to quilt back, backstitching at beginning of stitching and at mark (**Fig. 21**). Lift needle out of fabric and clip thread.

Fig. 20

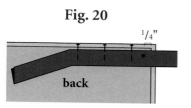

Fig. 21

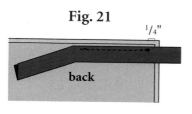

5 Fold binding as shown in **Figs. 22-23** and pin binding to adjacent side, matching raw edges. When reaching the next corner, mark ¹/₄" from edge of quilt back.

6 Backstitching at edge of quilt back, sew pinned binding to quilt back (**Fig. 24**); backstitch at the next mark. Lift needle out of fabric and clip thread.

7 Continue sewing binding to quilt back, stopping approximately 10" from starting point (**Fig. 25**).

8 Bring beginning and end of binding to center of opening and fold each end back, leaving a ¹/₄" space between folds (**Fig. 26**). Finger-press folds.

Fig. 22

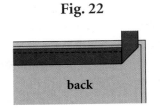

back

Fig. 23

back

Fig. 24

back

Fig. 25

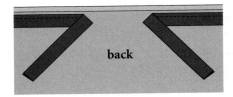

back

Fig. 26

back

9 Unfold ends of binding and draw a line across wrong side in finger-pressed crease. Draw a line through the lengthwise pressed fold of binding at same spot to create a cross mark. With edge of ruler at marked cross, line up 45° angle marking on ruler with one long side of binding. Draw a diagonal line from edge to edge. Repeat on remaining end, making sure that the two lines are angled the same way (**Fig. 27**).

10 Matching right sides and diagonal lines, pin binding ends together at right angles (**Fig. 28**).

11 Machine stitch along diagonal line, removing pins as you stitch (**Fig. 29**).

12 Lay binding against quilt to double-check that it is correct length.

13 Trim binding ends, leaving ¼" seam allowance; press seam allowances open. Stitch binding to quilt back.

14 On 1 edge of quilt, fold binding over to quilt front and pin pressed edge in place, covering stitching line (**Fig. 30**). On adjacent side, fold binding over, forming a mitered corner (**Fig. 31**). Repeat to pin remainder of binding in place.

15 Machine stitch binding in place.

Fig. 27

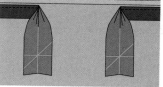

Fig. 28

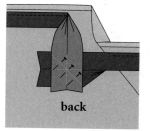

back

Fig. 29

Fig. 30

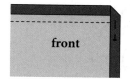

front

Fig. 31

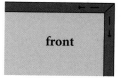

front

SPECIAL THANKS

My heartfelt thanks and appreciation go to Gay Molchen of Quilt Connection and Cheryl A. Schuller of the Quilting Asylum for their beautiful machine quilting.

I wish to give a special thanks to my friends, Susan Starcher, Marsha Walling, and Kelly Codispoti, at Jo-Ann Stores, Inc. who have so willingly shared their contacts and made my first book a reality.

I would like to thank Fabric Country, Princess Fabrics, RJR Fabrics, Spring Industries, Inc., VIP® by Cranston, and Sulky® of America for providing the supplies used in the quilts.

— *Cindy Casciato*

STANDARD MATTRESS AND QUILT SIZES

	Standard Mattress Sizes	Standard Quilt Sizes
Crib	27"x 52"	30"x 54"
Twin	39" x 75"	65" x 95"
Full	54" x 75"	80" x 95"
Queen	60" x 80"	86" x 100"
King	76" x 80"	106" x 106"

Metric Conversion Chart

Inches x 2.54 = centimeters (cm)	Yards x .9144 = meters (m)
Inches x 25.4 = millimeters (mm)	Yards x 91.44 = centimeters (cm)
Inches x .0254 = meters (m)	Centimeters x .3937 = inches (")
	Meters x 1.0936 = yards (yd)

Standard Equivalents

1/8"	3.2 mm	0.32 cm	1/8 yard	11.43 cm	0.11 m
1/4"	6.35 mm	0.635 cm	1/4 yard	22.86 cm	0.23 m
3/8"	9.5 mm	0.95 cm	3/8 yard	34.29 cm	0.34 m
1/2"	12.7 mm	1.27 cm	1/2 yard	45.72 cm	0.46 m
5/8"	15.9 mm	1.59 cm	5/8 yard	57.15 cm	0.57 m
3/4"	19.1 mm	1.91 cm	3/4 yard	68.58 cm	0.69 m
7/8"	22.2 mm	2.22 cm	7/8 yard	80 cm	0.8 m
1"	25.4 mm	2.54 cm	1 yard	91.44 cm	0.91 m